Lecture Notes in Computer Scien

T0238416

Commenced Publication in 1973
Founding and Former Series Editors:
Gerhard Goos, Juris Hartmanis, and Jan van Leeuwen

Nicolas Guelfi   Gianna Reggio
Alexander Romanovsky (Eds.)

Scientific Engineering of Distributed Java Applications

4th International Workshop, FIDJI 2004
Luxembourg-Kirchberg, Luxembourg, November 24-25, 2004
Revised Selected Papers

 Springer

Volume Editors

Nicolas Guelfi
University of Luxembourg
Faculty of Science, Technology and Communication
6, rue Richard Coudenhove-Kalergi, 1359 Luxembourg-Kirchberg, Luxembourg
E-mail: nicolas.guelfi@uni.lu

Gianna Reggio
University of Genoa
Department of Informatics
Via Dodecaneso 35, 16146 Genoa, Italy
E-mail: reggio@disi.unige.it

Alexander Romanovsky
University of Newcastle upon Tyne
School of Computing Science
Newcastle upon Tyne, NE1 7RU, UK
E-mail: alexander.romanovsky@ncl.ac.uk

Library of Congress Control Number: 2005921148

CR Subject Classification (1998): D.2, H.4, H.3, H.5.3-4, C.2.4, D.1.3

ISSN 0302-9743
ISBN 3-540-25053-0 Springer Berlin Heidelberg New York

Springer is a part of Springer Science+Business Media

springeronline.com

© Springer-Verlag Berlin Heidelberg 2005
Printed in Germany

Typesetting: Camera-ready by author, data conversion by Olgun Computergrafik
Printed on acid-free paper   SPIN: 11398066   06/3142   5 4 3 2 1 0

Preface

FIDJI 2004 has been an international forum for researchers and practitioners interested in the advances in, and applications of, software engineering for distributed application development. Concerning the technologies, the workshop focused on "Java-related" technologies. It was an opportunity to present and observe the latest research, results, and ideas in these areas.

All papers submitted to this workshop have been reviewed by at least two members of the International Program Committee. Acceptance has been based primarily on originality and contribution. We have selected, for these post-workshop proceedings, 11 papers amongst 22 submitted, a tutorial and two keynotes.

FIDJI 2004 aimed at promoting a scientific approach to software engineering. The scope of the workshop includes the following topics:
- design of distributed applications
- development methodologies for software and system engineering
- UML-based development methodologies
- development of reliable and secure distributed systems
- component-based development methodologies
- dependability support during system life cycle
- fault tolerance refinement, evolution and decomposition
- atomicity and exception handling in system development
- software architectures, frameworks and design patterns for developing distributed systems
- integration of formal techniques in the development process
- formal analysis and grounding of modelling notation and techniques (e.g.,UML, metamodelling)
- supporting the security and dependability requirements of distributed applications in the development process
- distributed software inspection
- refactoring methods
- industrial and academic case studies
- development and analysis tools

The organization of such a workshop represents an important amount of work. We would like to acknowledge all the program committee members, all the additional referees, all the organization committee members, the University of Luxembourg, Faculty of Science, Technology and Communication administrative, scientific and technical staff and the Henri-Tudor public research center.

FIDJI 2004 has mainly been supported by the "Ministère de l'enseignement supérieur et de la recherche" and by the "Fond National pour la Recherche au Luxembourg".

November 2004   Nicolas Guelfi, Gianna Reggio and Alexander Romanovsky
FIDJI 2004 chairs

Organization

FIDJI 2004 was organized by the University of Luxembourg, Faculty of Science, Technology and Communication.

Program Chairs

Guelfi, Nicolas	University of Luxembourg, Luxembourg
Reggio, Gianna	DISI Genoa, Italy
Romanovsky, Alexander	DCS, Newcastle, England

International Program Committee

Astesiano, Egidio	DISI Genoa, Italy
Biberstein, Olivier	Berne University of Applied Sciences, HTI, Bienne, Switzerland
Bouvry, Pascal	University of Luxembourg, Luxembourg
Di Marzo, Giovanna	CUI, Geneva, Switzerland
Dubois, Eric	CRP Henri-Tudor, Luxembourg
Fourdrinier, Frédéric	Hewlett-Packard, France
Gengler, Marc	ESIL, Marseille France
Guelfi, Nicolas	University of Luxembourg, Luxembourg
Guerraoui, Rachid	EPFL, Lausanne, Switzerland
Huzar, Zbigniew	Wroclaw University of Technology, Wroclaw, Poland
Keller, Rudolf	Zühlke Engineering, Schlieren, Switzerland
Kienzle, Jörg	McGill University, Montreal, Canada
Koskimies, Kai	University of Helsinki, Finland
Majzik, István	BUTE, Budapest, Hungary
Mammar, Amel	University of Luxembourg, Luxembourg
Molli, Pascal	LORIA, Nancy, France
Parnas, David	University of Limerick, Limerick, Ireland
Petitpierre, Claude	EPFL, Lausanne, Switzerland
Razavi, Reza	University of Luxembourg, Luxembourg
Reggio, Gianna	DISI, Genoa, Italy
Romanovsky, Sacha	DCS, Newcastle, England
Rothkugel, Steffen	University of Luxembourg, Luxembourg
Rottier, Geert	Hewlett-Packard, Belgium
Souquières, Jeanine	LORIA, Nancy, France
Troubitsyna, Elena	Aabo Akademi, Turku, Finland
Vachon, Julie	DIRO, Montreal, Canada
Warmer, Jos	De Nederlandsche Bank, Netherlands

Organizing Committee

Amza, Catalin	University of Luxembourg/DISI, Genoa, Italy
Berlizev, Andrey	University of Luxembourg, Luxembourg
Capozucca, Alfredo	University of Luxembourg, Luxembourg
Guelfi, Nicolas	University of Luxembourg, Luxembourg
Mammar, Amel	University of Luxembourg, Luxembourg
Perrouin, Gilles	University of Luxembourg, Luxembourg
Pruski, Cédric	University of Luxembourg, Luxembourg
Reggio, Gianna	DISI, Genoa, Italy
Ries, Angela	University of Luxembourg, Luxembourg
Ries, Benoît	University of Luxembourg, Luxembourg
Sterges, Paul	University of Luxembourg, Luxembourg

Additional Referees

Hnatkowska, Bogumila
Sterges, Paul

Sponsoring Institutions

This workshop has been supported by the University of Luxembourg, the Ministry for Culture, Higher Education and Research and the National Research Fund.

Table of Contents

Keynote Talks

Tutorials

Component-Based Design of Embedded Software:
An Analysis of Design Issues

Christo Angelov, Krzysztof Sierszecki, and Nicolae Marian

Mads Clausen Institute for Product Innovation, University of Southern Denmark
Grundtvigs Alle 150, 6400 Soenderborg, Denmark
{angelov,ksi,nicolae}@mci.sdu.dk

Abstract. Widespread use of embedded systems mandates the use of industrial production methods featuring model-based design and repositories of prefabricated software components. The main problem that has to be addressed in this context is to systematically develop a software architecture (framework) for embedded applications, taking into account the true nature of embedded systems, which are predominantly real-time control and monitoring systems. There are a great number of design issues and unresolved problems with existing architectures, which have to be carefully analyzed in order to develop a viable component-based design method for embedded applications. Such an analysis is presented in this paper, which focuses on a number of key issues: specification of system structure; specification of system behaviour; component scheduling and execution; program generation vs. system configuration. The analysis has been used to formulate the guidelines used to develop *COMDES* – a software framework for distributed embedded applications.

1 Introduction

The widespread use of embedded systems (including time-critical and safety-critical systems) poses a serious challenge to software developers in view of diverse, severe and conflicting requirements, e.g. reduced development and operating costs and reduced time to market, as well as specific issues that are particularly important for embedded systems: dependable operation through reliable and error-free software; predictable and guaranteed behaviour under hard real-time constraints; open architecture supporting software reuse and reconfiguration; architectural support for software scalability, including both stand-alone and distributed applications.

The above requirements cannot be met by currently used software technology, which is largely based on informal design methods and manual coding techniques. Recently, there have been successful attempts to overcome the above problem through model-based design and computer-aided generation of embedded software from high-level specifications. However, this approach has a serious drawback: it does not provide adequate support for dynamic (in-site and on-line) reconfiguration since it requires the generation and compilation of new code, which has to be subsequently downloaded into the target system. The ultimate solution to the above problem can be characterized as computer-aided *configuration* of embedded software using formal frameworks and pre-fabricated *executable* components. The latter may

N. Guelfi et al. (Eds.): FIDJI 2004, LNCS 3409, pp. 1–11, 2005.
© Springer-Verlag Berlin Heidelberg 2005

be implemented as re-locatable silicon libraries stored in non-volatile memory (ROM).

The main problem to be solved in this context is to develop a comprehensive framework that would reflect the true nature of embedded systems, which are predominantly real-time control and monitoring systems [16]. Developing such a framework and the associated software design method is a highly complex engineering task, which is currently in the focus of attention of many research groups but so far, there has been no widely accepted solution [16-26]. This is due to a number of factors: very high complexity, great diversity of applications and the absence of common approach towards embedded software development, which is further aggravated by the lack of previous research [17].

There are a great number of design issues and unresolved problems with existing architectures, which have to be carefully analyzed in order to develop a viable component-based design method for embedded applications. Such an analysis is presented in this paper, which focuses on a number of key issues: specification of system structure (section 2); specification of system behaviour (section 3); component scheduling and execution (section 4); program generation vs. system configuration (section 5). The analysis carried out has been used to define guidelines used to develop *COMDES* – a software framework for distributed embedded systems [2-4] whose main features are summarized in section 6.

2   Specification of System Structure

A great number of embedded systems use a *process-based* configuration specification in the context of static and/or dynamic process scheduling. A process-based system is conceived as a set of interacting processes (tasks) running under a real-time kernel or a static schedule. Process-based specifications are criticized for emphasizing the functional rather than the structural decomposition of real-time systems. Such specifications address naturally the problems of scheduling and schedulability analysis but the resulting solutions are usually far from being open and easily reconfigurable (especially in the case of static process scheduling).

Conversely, *object-based* specifications emphasize structural decomposition, which facilitates the implementation of open and reconfigurable systems, e.g. industrial software standards such as IEC 61131-3 [12] and IEC 61499 [13]. In that case the system is conceived as a composition of interacting components, such as function blocks and port-based objects, which are then mapped onto real-real-time tasks [13, 20], or alternatively – executed under a static schedule [24, 26]. Unfortunately, object-based design methods often disregard the problems of timing behaviour and schedulability analysis, which are of paramount importance for hard real time systems (e.g. the above two standards). There are some notable exceptions, however, e.g. HRT-HOOD, which has a sound foundation in modern Fixed-Priority Scheduling Theory [5].

Object-based design uses a number of fundamental principles such as encapsulation, aggregation and association of objects (components). Therefore, it is inherent to component-based design methods. However, a major problem that has to be overcome is the informal and largely ad-hoc definition of application objects. This can be observed in many software design methods, where it is left to the system designer to define system objects and object classes for each particular application. That applies not only to component functionality and interfacing, but also – to the way components are mapped onto real-time tasks (e.g. one component mapped onto one task [21, 24], several components mapped onto one task [13, 20], several tasks mapped onto one component [8, 11]).

It can be argued that a software design method should incorporate both types of specification into a hierarchical model, taking into account both the structural and computational aspects of system architecture. This has resulted in the development of hybrid architectures and design methods such as ARTS [8] and SDL [11] that are both object and process-based. That is, the system is conceived as a composition of active objects, each of them encapsulating one or more threads of control. Threads invoke the operations of passive objects and the latter may invoke the operations of other objects, etc. This approach results in well-structured systems, featuring a well-specified hierarchy of active and passive objects, but once again, these are defined by the system designer for each particular case.

Ad-hoc specification and design severely limits component reusability. Therefore, it is necessary to develop a formal framework that will allow for a *systematic* specification of reconfigurable components, which will be reusable by definition. The proper way of doing this is to specify software components using decomposition criteria that are derived from the areas of control engineering and systems science rather than human experience and intuition, taking into account that modern embedded systems are predominantly control and monitoring systems [16].

This has been achieved to some extent in industrial software standards (e.g. those mentioned above) but at a relatively low level, i.e. the level of passive objects such as function blocks [12, 13]. However, no provision is made for reconfigurable state machines or hybrid models involving reconfigurable state machines and function blocks. Conversely, there are a few systems featuring reconfigurable state machines, e.g. AIRES [20] and StateWORKS [23], but they do not provide support for function blocks and function block diagrams in the sense of IEC 61131-3 and similar standards.

Component interaction is another major issue that has to be resolved while specifying system configuration. There are a number of interaction patterns, which are widely used in the context of both process-based and object-based systems: client-server, producer-consumer(s) and publisher-subscribers. Client-server is highly popular in the IT community and is also used in industrial computer systems and protocols. However, it has limitations, such as the blocking nature of communication and point-to-point interactions. Therefore, producer-consumer is considered better suited for real-time systems because it is non-blocking and supports one-to-many interactions [7]. Publisher-subscriber combines the useful features of the former two methods and it is also widely used in practice.

The above patterns can be implemented via component interfaces, which are defined in the component interface model. Embedded systems use basically two types of such models: a) the IEC 61131 type of model specifying component interfaces in terms of signal inputs and outputs, whereby a component output is directly linked to one or more inputs of other components (function blocks); b) port-based objects interacting via suitably linked input and output ports that are implemented as shared memory locations. The latter model has been specifically developed for robotics applications [21] but similar models have been widely used in other application domains as well, e.g. ROOM [10], SDL [11], SOFIA [22], PECOS [25], etc. Port-based objects provide a high degree of flexibility but at the same time their use may result in relatively complex models (diagram clutter) because it is necessary to explicitly specify all ports and port connections for a given application.

This problem is overcome in IEC 61131-like models through implicit definition of I/O buffers and softwiring of inputs and outputs resulting in simple and easy to understand models – function block diagrams [12]. In this case I/O buffers are defined within the corresponding execution records of interconnected function block instances, whereby an input variable value can be obtained from the corresponding output using either an I/O assignment statement, or even better – a pointer specifying the source of data for the corresponding input-to-output connection. However, this technique is directly applicable to low-level components such as function blocks but it does not scale up well to distributed applications. It the latter case, it is necessary to use special-purpose components, e.g. service interface function blocks [13], with the resulting loss of transparency.

Distributed applications require higher-level components (function units). These are software agents implementing autonomous subsystems, such as sensor, controller, actuator, etc., that are usually allocated to different network nodes and interact with one another within various types of distributed transactions. Therefore, the basic control engineering approach has to be extended into a *systems engineering approach,* in order to take into account the complexity of real-world applications. Accordingly, it is necessary to extend the softwiring technique, so that function units are connected with each other in a uniform manner and signals are exchanged *transparently* between them, independent of their physical allocation. This would require the development of a special-purpose protocol supporting the transparent exchange of signals, i.e. labeled messages, between interacting function units [1].

3   Specification of System Behaviour

At the operational level of specification, there is a controversy between various paradigms, e.g. event-driven vs. time-driven operation and control flow vs. data flow models. Consequently, some architectures and design methods emphasize event-driven reactive behavior and control flow, whereas others focus on time-driven operation and the data flow between interacting components and subsystems. The former type of software architecture is usually associated with discontinuous event-driven systems, whereas the latter is preferred with continuous control systems. This situation reflects a gap between continuous and discontinuous systems modeling and design (e.g. state machines vs. data flow diagrams), which has been recognized by the control engineering community.

However, such a differentiation of system models is largely artificial and it clearly comes into conflict with the nature of real plants, which are more or less hybrid, even if they are treated as predominantly discrete or continuous. That is even more obvious in the case of complex hybrid control systems and applications. On the other hand, it can be shown that a sequential control system can be represented with a function block diagram (in terms of gates and flip-flops) and likewise – a continuous control system can be entirely specified in terms of state machines, even though these are not perhaps the typical modeling techniques for the above two types of system.

Similarly, a discontinuous event-driven system can be specified and implemented as a time-driven synchronous state machine; on the other hand, time-driven behaviour can be considered a special case of event-driven behaviour, where periodic activities are triggered by regularly arriving timing events, e.g. *timeout* events as defined in Statecharts.

Synchronous time-driven implementation is actually preferred by real-time engineers, because such systems have periodic task execution patterns, and this is a major prerequisite for the estimation of task response times using analysis techniques developed in modern Real-Time Scheduling Theory. It is worth noting that synchronous time-driven systems are preferred not only by real-time engineers but also, by control engineers: most practical examples of industrial control systems – both continuous and sequential – are synchronous systems triggered by periodically arriving timing events.

That is also the choice of hardware engineers, who implement sequential circuits as synchronous (clock-driven) state machines. However, this example prompts another interesting observation: hardware systems generate signals (i.e. reactions to timing events) with a very small delay, which can be ignored for the purpose of analysis. That is, it is possible to assume zero delay between the clock event and the corresponding reaction. This is the well-known *synchrony hypothesis*, which has been also adopted for a class of real time systems in a more general event-driven context, assuming that events are clocked and subsequently processed by the system before the next tick arrives. There are a number of architectures and programming languages illustrating this approach, e.g. real-time languages such as ESTEREL, LUSTRE, and SIGNAL [9]. However, these languages use an interleaved model of execution, whereby concurrent processes (state machines) are compiled into sequential programs with the resulting loss of modularity [18].

The above discussion has outlined the duality of various paradigms used to specify system behaviour. Nonetheless, there is seemingly no model combining naturally the reactive and the transformational aspects of system behavior, both of which are inherent to real-world systems and especially – to complex hybrid control systems. There have been attempts to solve this problem, and most notably the MoBIES project being developed at the University of California, Berkeley [18]. That project combines numerous computational models into a hybrid object-oriented framework, whereby the notion of computational model includes not only "pure" operational models such as state machines and data flow diagrams, but also – process interaction and execution models. Unfortunately, this has resulted in an overly complex framework featuring multiple operational domains and "polymorphic" component interfaces, which seems to be too complicated for practical purposes. This framework is supported by an equally complex software engineering environment featuring a multi-stage program generation process.

Another attempt to bridge the gap between event-driven and time-driven behaviour and accordingly – between control flow and data flow, is illustrated with the component model introduced in standard IEC 61499 [13]. In that case reactive (event-driven) and data transformation aspects are combined into low-level components such as function blocks. Whereas this is a big step forward in comparison with the previous standard IEC 61131-3 [12], it has also substantial limitations: for each function block, event-driven behaviour is specified in terms of a limited subset of input and output events that are defined in the interface specification of the function block. Accordingly, event-driven behaviour is specified with a state transition graph, which is "hardwired" in the function block. Hence, it is impossible to reconfigure the state machine, without re-designing and re-implementing the function block.

This limits substantially component reusability, since in the general case a function block may be expected to execute in different contexts, e.g. operational modes of a complex modal controller whose behaviour is specified with a state transition graph that is different from the one encoded in the function block. On the other hand, it might be possible to execute a sequence of function blocks within a given mode of operation. Hence, it is not necessary to replicate the state transition graph in all function blocks involved, which could result in undue overhead.

Instead, state transition logic might be implemented within a higher level of abstraction, i.e. a state machine that would be capable of executing function blocks and/or function block sequences (function block diagrams) within different states/modes of operation. This is essentially a hybrid state machine, which combines in a natural way the reactive and transformational aspects of component behaviour. It can be eventually encapsulated into a function block of class *reconfigurable state machine*, which can be used to implement complex behaviour for a broad range of embedded applications.

4 Component Scheduling and Execution

Component operations are mapped onto real-time processes (tasks) that have to be executed concurrently in a multi-tasking and possibly – multiple-node distributed environment. This is related to another aspect of operational behaviour, i.e. process scheduling and execution, which has to be provided by some kind of operational environment, guaranteeing that processes are executed within specified deadlines. This problem is further complicated when processes are executed as integral part of (possibly complex) sequences – transactions, which have to satisfy the corresponding end-to-end deadlines. It becomes even more complex in the case of distributed transactions, where computational and communication tasks have to be executed in different scheduling domains – network nodes, communication media, etc., observing once again the corresponding end-to-end deadlines. However, in all cases the adopted scheduling mechanism has to provide a safe operational environment for application tasks, i.e. predictable and guaranteed behaviour under hard real-time constraints.

There are basically two approaches to process scheduling for dependable embedded systems: *static scheduling* vs. predictable *dynamic scheduling* using algorithms developed in modern Real-Time Scheduling Theory. Static scheduling is widely used with dependable real-time systems in application areas such as aerospace and military systems, automotive applications, etc., and it is illustrated with the timed-triggered architecture specifically developed for this type of system [7]. It has also been used with a number of component-based design methods as well, see e.g. [24, 26]. However, this approach has a major disadvantage: its use results in closed systems that are generally difficult to re-configure and maintain. This is in contradiction to another requirement – the widespread use of embedded systems mandates the development of open systems supporting large-scale software reuse as well as in-site and on-line re-configuration.

Dynamic scheduling is more promising, as illustrated by recent developments such as the Ada Ravenscar Profile, which defines guidelines for predictable task execution and interaction in the context of preemptive priority-based scheduling [15]. However, this approach requires the development of a new generation of so-called *safe* real-time kernels, which provide a secure and predictable environment for application tasks through a number of specific features: predictable task scheduling, safe task interaction, extensive timing and monitoring facilities, and finally – predictable kernel behaviour. However, it has to be pointed out that available real-time kernels (with the exception of a few experimental designs) do not satisfy the above requirements. For example, most of them are implemented using linked-list queues resulting in substantial and largely varying overhead, i.e. kernel jitter [6]. The elimination of kernel jitter will make it possible to accurately estimate task and transaction response times early in the design process taking into account kernel execution effects, as illustrated by the HARTEX family of real-time kernels [1, 4].

On the other hand, jitter-free operation can be eventually extended to application tasks by enforcing their execution within worst-case execution time bounds. That will ultimately result in highly predictable and reproducible system behaviour and consequently – greatly enhanced system testability [14]. Another option is to combine static and dynamic scheduling within a hybrid real-time kernel, e.g. RUBUS [24].

However, a much better approach has recently emerged, i.e. *timed multitasking* – a powerful yet elegant and conceptually simple model of computation [19]. Under that model task I/O drivers are invoked and executed atomically at precisely specified time instants (i.e. task release and deadline instants), whereas application tasks are executed in a preemptive priority-driven environment and may have termination jitter. However, jitter is effectively eliminated as long as tasks finish execution before their deadlines. This makes it possible to engineer real-time systems that combine high flexibility inherent to dynamic scheduling with predictable jitter-free operation, which is typical for statically scheduled systems.

5   Program Generation vs. System Configuration

Two approaches to component-based design of embedded systems have recently emerged. The first one follows a more conventional development line, which started with executable models and rapid prototyping systems. It can be characterized as computer-aided generation of embedded software using frameworks and source-code component libraries. This approach is illustrated by a number of research projects and commercial systems, e.g. Rhapsody®, Rose/RT®, etc.

However, program generation has a serious drawback: it does not provide adequate support for system reconfiguration, since it requires the generation and compilation of new code, which has to be subsequently downloaded into the target system. Moreover, this proces has been strongly biased by existing design methods and languages (e.g. UML/C++), resulting in solutions that are most often intended for high-end systems having a lot of processing power and memory. There are some tools that can be used with low-end microcontrollers, such as the IAR visualSTATE®, which generates C code out of UML state diagrams. Unfortunately, it uses an interleaved model of execution, which does not provide adequate support for modularity and hard real-time operation.

The second approach follows a development line that started with some industrial automation systems a few decades ago. It can be characterized as computer-aided *configuration* of embedded software using formal frameworks and pre-fabricated *executable* components. The latter may be implemented as re-locatable *silicon libraries* stored in non-volatile memory, whereby each component is specified in terms of functional characteristics and resource requirements (e.g. memory usage and execution time for a given type of micro-controller). In that case configuration data is stored in RAM-resident data structures (tables) that comprise the real-time database of the application. With this type of system, program generation is used in a limited manner in order to generate code for low-level components such as basic function blocks, to be included in the component library.

This approach has been used in some recent developments featuring reconfigurable state machines, e.g. StateWORKS [23], but this environment does not provide support for function blocks and function block diagrams. Another example is the SOFIA framework [22]. However, the latter is limited to continuous systems specified in terms of object diagrams and port-based objects.

Software configuration is obviously the better choice in terms of quality of service and the prerequisites that are needed to make a transition to the industrial production stage of embedded software development. Its main advantage is the inherent support for system reconfiguration, which is achieved by updating data structures whereas executable codes remain unchanged.

The importance of system reconfiguration (including in-site and on-line re-configuration) has been recently emphasized by the latest trends and requirements in the area of embedded systems (see [27] for a detailed discussion). It can be implemented off-line, i.e. before the system is restarted or eventually – on line, during system operation. On-line reconfiguration has been studied by a number of research groups [21, 22, 27]. However, this is a complex problem that has to be treated with caution, especially in safety-critical systems, and further research is needed in a number of areas: 1) Specific issues that have to be addressed in the context of dynamically scheduled systems, such as mode-change protocols, replica determinism, etc.; 2) Fundamental problems of system safety and dynamics during reconfiguration, which go beyond the basic issues of software reconfiguration, e.g. system stability, bumpless transfer of control during mode changes, etc.

6   A Software Framework for Distributed Embedded Systems

The guidelines formulated in the preceding discussion have been used to develop COMDES [2-4] – a software framework for distributed embedded applications whose main features are briefly summarized below:

- The distributed embedded system is conceived as a composition of *function units*,
  i.e. software agents that correspond to autonomous subsystems, such as sensor, ac-

tuator, controller, operator station, etc. Function units may be viewed as large-scale software integrated circuits that have to be *softwired* with one another in order to configure specific applications.

- Function units encapsulate one or more threads of control *(activities)*. These are composed from prefabricated software components *(function blocks)* implementing standard signal processing and control functions. Activities are specified with function block diagrams, i.e. acyclic signal flow graphs that can be ultimately encapsulated into higher-order *(composite)* function blocks.

- Complex activity behaviour is specified in terms of *hybrid state machines* – a hierarchical executable model that takes into account both the reactive and transformational aspects of system behaviour. Hence, it can be used to specify a broad range of embedded applications, such as discrete, continuous and hybrid control systems, signal processing systems, etc. That model has been ultimately implemented as a reconfigurable function block of class state machine.

- Function units interact by exchanging *signals*, i.e. messages having unique communication variable identifiers (e.g. temperature, pressure, etc.). Signals are exchanged by means of input and output *signal drivers* – a special class of function blocks that are used to communicate with the outside world and other function units. These implement a softwiring protocol providing for transparent communication between function units, independent of their allocation on network nodes. Signal drivers are conceived as interface components of a software integrated circuit (by analogy with hardware integrated circuits), which are automatically instantiated when a function unit is configured.

- Signal drivers may be viewed as a special class of I/O drivers within the timed multitasking model of computation. Accordingly, they can be invoked at precisely specified time instants resulting in time-triggered communication between subsystems (function units) and encapsulated activities. Alternatively, it is possible to invoke signal drivers at the beginning and at the end of activity execution, which is typical for event-triggered communication and phase-aligned transactions.

- These techniques can be used to implement various types of distributed transactions, e.g. phase-aligned transactions, time-triggered transactions with precisely specified input/output and activity release times, and any combination thereof, in the context of the *timed multitasking* model of computation. The latter is currently supported by the latest timed-multitasking version of the HARTEX kernel [4].

More information can be found in the quoted sources, as well as other papers and documents that can be downloaded from http://seg.msi.sdu.dk.

7 Conclusion

The presented analysis has outlined the requirements that have to be satisfied by an embedded system framework: The framework must support an open software architecture through a well-defined hierarchy of reusable and reconfigurable components. On the other hand, it must support predictable and deterministic behaviour in time critical and safety-critical applications without sacrificing flexibility. At the operational level, the framework has to provide models capable of adequately specifying system behaviour for a broad range of sequential, continuous and hybrid applications. Last but not least, the modeling techniques and notations used must be intuitive and easy to understand by application domain experts.

These guidelines have been instrumental in developing the COMDES framework, which defines a hierarchy of reusable executable components, such as basic and composite function blocks, reconfigurable state machines, activities and function units. The main innovation of the framework is the non-conventional definition of component objects and object interactions. Software objects, e.g. function units, emulate integrated circuits and interact by exchanging signals. Hence, it is not necessary to explicitly specify their interfaces in terms of invoked operations or artefacts such as I/O ports, message objects, etc. Consequently, changes in function unit structure and allocation do not affect the internal structure and operation of other function units, as long as signal flow and transaction dynamics are preserved. This feature facilitates system reconfiguration and provides for transparent communication between function units, which will ultimately facilitate the engineering of flexible and truly open distributed embedded systems.

The adopted system model has been further elaborated using function units with time-triggered inputs and outputs, in the context of the timed multitasking model of computation. This makes it possible to engineer component-based systems that combine high flexibility inherent to dynamically scheduled systems and predictable jitter-free operation, which is usually associated with their statically scheduled counterparts.

References

1. Angelov, C., Ivanov, I., Burns, I.: HARTEX – a Safe Real-Time Kernel for Distributed Computer Control Systems. Software: Practice and Experience, vol. 32, N 3, March (2002) 209-232
2. Angelov, C., Sierszecki, K.: Component-based Design of Software for Distributed Embedded Systems. Proc. The 10th IEEE International Conference on Methods and Models in Automation and Robotics, Miedzyzdroje, Poland (2004)
3. Angelov, C., Sierszecki, K.: A Software Framework for Component-Based Embedded Applications. To be presented to APSEC'2004, November (2004)
4. Angelov, C., Berthing, C., Sierszecki, C., Marian, N.: Function Unit Specification in a Timed Multitasking Environment. To be presented to ICSSEA'2004, Paris, France, December (2004)
5. Burns, A., Wellings, A.J.: HRT-HOOD: A Design Method for Hard Real-Time Ada. Real-Time Systems, vol. 6, No 1 (1994) 73-114
6. Burns, A., Tindell, A., Wellings, A.: Effective analysis for engineering real-time fixed-priority schedulers. IEEE Trans. on Soft. Eng., vol. 21 (1995) 475-480
7. Kopetz, H., Bauer, G.: The Time-Triggered Architecture. Proceedings of the IEEE, Special Issue on Embedded Systems, June (2002)
8. Mercer, C., Tokuda, H.: The ARTS Real-Time Object Model. Proc. of the IEEE Real-Time Systems Symposium (1990) 2-10
9. Benveniste, A., Berry, G.: The Synchronous Approach to Reactive and Real-Time Systems. Proc. of the IEEE, vol. 79, No 9 (1991) 1270-1282

10. Selic, B., Gullegson, G., Ward, P.T.: Real-Time Object-Oriented Modeling. John Wiley & Sons (1994)
11. Faergemand, O., Olsen, A.: Introduction to SDL-92. Computer Networks and ISDN Systems, vol 26 (1994) 1143-1167
12. John, K.H., Tiegelkamp, M.: IEC 61131-3: Programming Industrial Automation Systems. Springer (2001)
13. Lewis, R.: Modeling Control Systems Using IEC 61499. Institution of Electrical Engineers (2001)
14. Thane, H., Pettersson, A., Sundmark, D.: The Asterix Real-Time Kernel. Proc. of the 13th Euromicro International Conference On Real-Time Systems, Delft, Netherlands (2001)
15. Burns, A., Dobbing, B., Vardanega, T.: Guide for the Use of the Ada Ravenscar Profile in High Integrity Systems. University of York Technical Report YCS-2003-348, January (2003)
16. Software Technologies, Embedded Systems and Distributed Systems in FP6. Workshop on Software Technologies, Embedded Systems and Distributed Systems in the 6th Framework Programme for EU Research, Brussels, Belgium, May (2002)
17. Lee, E.: What's Ahead for Embedded Software. IEEE Computer, 2000, N 9, (2000) 18-26
18. Lee, E.: Embedded Software – an Agenda for Research. UCB ERL Memorandum M99/63, University of California at Berkeley, December (1999)
19. Liu, J., Lee, E. A.: Timed Multitasking for Real-Time Embedded Software. IEEE Control Systems Magazine: Advances in Software Enabled Control, February (2003) 65-75
20. Wang, S., Shin, K.G.: An Architecture for Embedded Software Integration Using Reusable Components. Proc. of the International Conference on Compilers, Architecture, and Synthesis for Embedded Systems, San Jose, CA (2000)
21. Stewart, D.B., Volpe, R.A., Khosla, P.K.: Design of Dynamically Reconfigurable Real-Time Software Using Port-Based Objects. IEEE Trans. on Soft. Eng., vol.23, No 12 (1997) 759-776
22. Zimmermann, U., Längle, T., Wörn, T.: Online Software Reconfiguration in Embedded Real-Time Control Systems. Proc. of the SCI 2002, vol. VI (2002) 375-379
23. Wagner, F., Wolstenholme, P.: Modeling and Building Reliable, Reusable Software. Proc. of the 10th IEEE International Conference and Workshop on the Engineering of Computer-Based Systems (2003)
24. Isovic, D., Norström, C.: Components in Real-Time Systems. Proc. of the 8th International Conference on Real-Time Computing Systems and Applications, Tokyo, Japan (2002)
25. Nierstrasz, O. et al.: A Component Model for Field Devices. Proc. of the IFIP/ACM Working Conference on Component Deployment, Germany (2002)
26. Gunzert, M.: Building Safety-Critical Real-Time Systems with Synchronous Software Components. Proc. of the Joint IFAC/IFIP WRTP'99 and ARTDB'99 Workshop, Germany (1999)
27. Stewart, D.B., Arora, G.: Dynamically Reconfigurable Embedded Software – Does It Make Sense? Proc. of the 2nd IEEE International Conference on Engineering of Complex Computer Systems and Real-Time Applications Workshop, Montreal, Canada (1996) 217-220

How Design Patterns Affect
Application Performance –
A Case of a Multi-tier J2EE Application

Jakub Rudzki

Solita Oy, Hermiankatu 1, 33720 Tampere, Finland
jakub.rudzki@solita.fi

Abstract. Different kinds of patterns, especially design patterns, are popular and useful concepts in software engineering. In some cases, flexibility and reusability of the design comes with the price of decreased efficiency. At the same time, performance is often a key quality attribute of distributed applications. It is therefore beneficial to investigate whether design patterns may influence performance of applications. This paper investigates differences in performance between selected design patterns implemented in an example multi-tier J2EE application.

To this end, a series of performance tests in distinctive Enterprise Java Beans containers and deployment configurations were carried out. The comparison of the differences between results for each tested design pattern indicates influence on application quality, especially performance.

Keywords: Design patterns, J2EE, Performance, Application quality.

1   Introduction

The concept of design patterns [1] has been present in software engineering for a relatively long time. Design patterns function in software engineering along with other pattern categories, for instance, reengineering patterns [2] or analysis patterns [3]. The use of patterns may improve software quality by making it more reusable, maintainable, and comprehensible. In addition, developers are increasingly more aware of how and when to use different kinds of patterns.

In an ideal world merely the architectural aspects of design patterns would determine how they should be used to create a software system. However, in the real world of software development there is seldom freedom to consider only architectural details of design patterns. Instead, factors like already existing parts of the software system impose requirements and restrictions that must also be taken into account. Additionally, the customers may have requirements and expectations about the deployment platform when making an order. These factors may affect the original design decisions. This paper investigates influences of design decisions, focusing on selected design patterns, on *performance*. The comparison of test results presented can be used as initial guidelines on design pattern usage with respect to performance and quality of multi-tier applications,

N. Guelfi et al. (Eds.): FIDJI 2004, LNCS 3409, pp. 12–23, 2005.

in particular in web applications developed in Java 2 Enterprise Edition (J2EE) technology [4].

Performance of an application is particularly important for a customer ordering a piece of software. Usually, it is not essential for the client to know what kinds of architectural decisions were made. However, it is far more important to know how the software performs, whether its services are reliable and available for end-users as expected. The quality requirements for an on-line shop or a banking system will most likely be different from those for an intranet portal presenting company news. In order to set and later meet the quality requirements, it is essential to clearly define them first. Performance is an important external quality attribute, which can be measured as *throughput* expressed by the number of requests the application serves per unit of time. However, performance is only one of many parameters of an application that determine the quality of the final product. In addition to that, performance-related aspects can be characterised by average response time, rate of correctly handled requests, and number of requests for which the handling time exceeds a certain level. All these parameters combined together can give a comprehensive view of the behaviour of an application.

A lot of suggestions how design patterns could be utilised have been presented in the literature. For instance, Gamma et al. present a pattern catalogue and discuss the applicability of each design pattern [2]. In addition, various authors describe patterns specific to a particular technology, for example [3,4]. Many of those patterns are based on the ones described by Gamma et al. while some of the solutions can be implemented only in a given technology. There is also a number of publications on the performance of J2EE containers. The differences between particular J2EE containers and some design solutions in the application implementation are investigated in [5–7]. Additionally, testing techniques are presented in [8, 9].

This paper presents supplementary implications of the use of design patterns in particular environments. The discussed design choices do not contradict each other, rather, they can be regarded as equivalent replacements from the functional point of view. The tests are focused not only on performance alone, but also on other quality factors of the application. In addition, the test application reflects a typical complexity level of commercial implementations, while managing a fairly large amount of data. This ensures relevance of obtained results to real-life applications. The test application is a simple Document Version Control (DVC) system, which allows users to store documents, restrict access to them, and keep track of changes. A more detailed description of the application is presented in Section 2.1.

The tests consider one case where a design pattern used to provide access to the business layer, is replaced by another design pattern in the example application. The chosen patterns were Facade and Command [1] implemented in the J2EE technology. The choice of the two design patterns was not arbitrary; an architect of a software system could face this kind of choice during the design process. These two design patterns are widely used to provide access to services in a business tier of a multi-tier application. Therefore, guidelines indicating benefits and drawbacks of each pattern in a particular deployment environment could improve the final product in terms of performance.

The test environment is presented in Section 2. It first introduces the example application, highlighting the design patterns used. After that, the measurement methodology and test environment are discussed. The test results and the analysis of these are presented in Sections 3 and 4. Finally, concluding remarks are presented in Section 5.

2   The Test Environment

2.1   The Example Application – Document Version Control System

The key functionality of the Document Version Control system, chosen as the test application, includes document storage, version control, and access control. This application is complex enough to be comparable with typical multi-tier applications and yet reasonably simple to implement and test. The application is built as a three-layer J2EE application. The presentation layer (web user interface) consists of a servlet and a few Java Server Pages (JSP). A set of session and entity beans providing the application services constitutes the business layer. Finally, the underlying database provides a persistent storage for application data. The simplified application architecture and deployment examples used in this experiment are shown in Figures 1(a) and 1(b).

The two patterns used alternatively during the tests were located in the business logic layer and were a connection point to the presentation layer. The choice of the Facade and Command patterns was dictated by their similar functionality from the presentation layer point of view. The selected patterns were implemented in the J2EE technology as described in [10]. The Facade design pattern provides a set of methods that a client can call to get access to services offered by the business layer. While the Command pattern is based on the concept of abstract command (a plain Java class) that can be executed to access business layer services. Depending on how the command class is implemented it allows the client to set certain parameters and execute the command in a command executor that is located in the business layer. After completing the

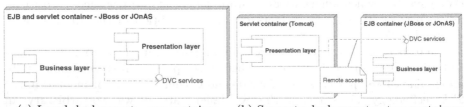

(a) Local deployment - one container   (b) Separate deployments - two cantainers

Fig. 1. Deployments

command execution, the client can retrieve results from the instance of the command class. Both patterns provide access to application services while hiding the complexity of the underlying implementation. Moreover, using the patterns reduces the number of calls to the entity beans when compared to a situation where a client calls all application beans directly. The significance of the call reduction has been described by many authors, for instance, in [11, 10, 5]. It is possible to imagine an implementation where a Command corresponds to a method provided by a Facade. In that case, there is not the overhead due to additional calls. In addition to the Command and Facade patterns, a modified Command design pattern was used; the modification focused on executing not only one command at a time, but if possible, more commands. The multiple executions clearly save additional network calls but require more handling at the client and server side (the presentation and business layers). The modified Command, later referred to as 'Command Combined', is particularly useful when an update operation is executed and after that the updated data is fetched to the presentation layer.

2.2   Measurement Methodology

In this paper, the quality of an application is considered from performance point of view. The metrics used include the following:

- the number of requests that the application is able to serve within a specified unit of time (throughput),
- response time measured by the time a client sending a request has to wait for the response,
- reliability measured as a number of correctly served requests, and
- the number of requests, the processing time of which is longer than a threshold value.

In order to measure all the above parameters of the example application, JMeter tool version 1.9 [12] was used. That tool can send a number of requests that simulate an active user of the application. By collecting information on the response time and content, it is possible to calculate all the above-mentioned metrics. As the test data was gathered in XML files, XSLT templates were used to process the data into a form used in analysis. The templates used in the tests were based on [13].

The test scenario included activities typical for this kind of applications:

- logging in to the application,
- listing accessible documents,
- downloading the content of a certain document,
- creating and deleting a private group of users allowed to access some of the documents, and
- adding and removing users from the private group.

The documents that were used in those operations were externally generated and inserted to the database.

All the activities were simulated with a number of concurrent users increasing from five to 220. This final number of users was determined empirically and it was the maximum number of users that the application and server could handle. After running a full sequence of requests for given number of users, it was repeated until the total number of requests reached around 18 000 requests. This number was also determined empirically and it was when the response time from the server was stable, meaning that the server had already allocated enough resources to serve a given number of users.

A test round for one tested case started from simulating 5 concurrent users. Then the number was set to 10 users and after that it was always increased by 10 until the maximum number of 220 users was reached. Each round was repeated 4 times to ensure that the results are meaningful and reliable.

2.3 Deployment Platforms

The test application was deployed on two popular open source Enterprise Java Bean (EJB) containers. An EJB container provides services to an application that is deployed on the container. The provided services include security, transaction management, and the persistent storage of data. The first container used was JBoss version 3.2 [14] and the second one was JOnAS version 4.1 [15]. In both cases the persistent state was stored in a MySQL database [16], which used transactional tables. The reason for enabling transactions at the database level was dictated by a possibility of corrupted data in the case of application failures. This kind of setting reflects a usual database configuration in web applications dealing with sensitive data. All deployment components had a default configuration apart from the transactional tables in the case of the MySQL database, and increased Java Virtual Machine heap size to 512 MB. The database was populated with data simulating 500 unique users and 1500 uploaded documents (3 per user).

Since the test cases included also a remote access to the application, a Tomcat servlet container version 5.0 [17] was used. In those cases, the presentation layer was deployed on the Tomcat container and the business logic layer was deployed on JBoss or JOnAS container.

In all test cases, the database and containers were located on one node, a machine with two P4 2.4 GHz processors, 1 GB RAM, 80 GB disc space and 100 Mb network card run under Windows XP Professional. The separation of nodes would increase network traffic and lower the response times, however, in the test cases the actual values were not the main concern, rather the differences between the cases were of interest. Therefore, one node was sufficient. The test client (JMeter) was located on a separate node within the same local network.

3 General Findings

Some general findings concerning all the application variants can be identified. The first finding concerns the case of local deployment, where both presentation

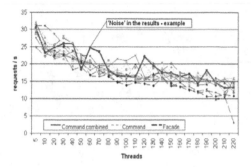

Fig. 2. Throughput values for Command Combined, Command, and Facade patterns in the case of local deployment on JBoss

and business layers are deployed on the same container. The obtained results contain quite a bit of 'noise', i.e., a relatively large number of results do not correlate with other results gathered for the same test case. Fig. 2 illustrates the average amount of noise encountered when using Command Combined, Command, and Facade patterns in the case of local deployments on JBoss. The throughput curves for all tested patterns are very irregular and it is not possible to observe noticeable differences between them.

In many cases the throughput values decrease rapidly just to increase for the next measurement point, which is defined for each number of simulated users. That behaviour can be seen in Fig. 2. Throughput for Command Combined, for example, for 40 users is above 25 requests per second (req/sec), for the next measurement point for 50 users the throughput decreases to under 20 req/sec. Finally for 60 users, the throughput increases back to almost 25 req/sec.

On the other hand, in the case of separately deployed presentation and business layers, on two separate containers, the results are much more correlated. This is illustrated in Figures 3(a) and 3(b). The differences between local and separate deployments were observed regardless of the container type.

Furthermore, in all the cases there is a clearly identifiable point when the application cannot handle more load. That happens when the number of clients reaches around 150. This is depicted in Fig. 4(b). Additionally, when the container cannot handle the increased number of requests and returns error responses, the performance improves. That behaviour is caused by the fact that requests causing errors are not processed entirely. They are, therefore, handled much quicker.

As it could be expected, the performance of the application deployed on a single container (locally) is much higher than when the presentation and business layers are separated. This can be concluded from Figures 2 and 3(a).

There are also differences between the containers. Application deployed separately on JOnAS, shown in Fig. 3(b), could handle almost twice as much requests per second as the application deployed on JBoss, shown in Fig. 3(a).

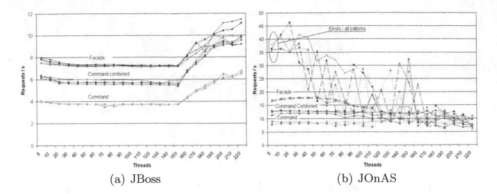

(a) JBoss   (b) JOnAS

Fig. 3. Throughput values in the case of separate presentation layer and business layer deployments

4 Detailed Results

4.1 Facade

The throughput of the application with Facade pattern deployed on a single container is similar in cases of JBoss and JOnAS. The only difference between the containers is a more steeply decreasing throughput line, in the case of JBoss (Fig. 4(a)). Additionally, separately deployed applications have much flatter characteristic of throughput with respect to the increasing number of requests.

The average response time is increasing almost linearly in all the deployment cases along with increasing number of clients. This is illustrated in Fig. 4(b). However, in the case of JBoss the average response time reaches the peak of 20 000 ms for 150 clients, which is the break point where the container cannot serve more users.

The rate of successful requests has similar characteristics for all the cases. In the beginning it is nearly 100%, while after reaching the break point, the rate drops. The drop in the case of separately deployed application layers is rather clear and rapid, as can be seen in Fig. 4(c). It is also worth noticing that in the case of separate deployments on JOnAS, the rate drops to almost 16% for about 110 concurrent users. However, in the consecutive rounds it does not start from expected level of around 100%. A reason for that behaviour could be an excessive number of transactions that had been started in the previous test round and did not complete until the next test round causing the handling of requests to fail. Since that situation is observed for all the design patterns, it does not affect overall comparison of the patterns. This disturbance is present in all figures referring to the case of separate deployment on JOnAS, for example, in Fig. 3(b) where it is marked with the label "Errors - all patterns".

Additionally, in the case of locally deployed application on JBoss, the noise is very significant from the very beginning, as can be seen in Fig. 4(c). The success rate varies even before reaching the break point where the success rate decreases significantly.

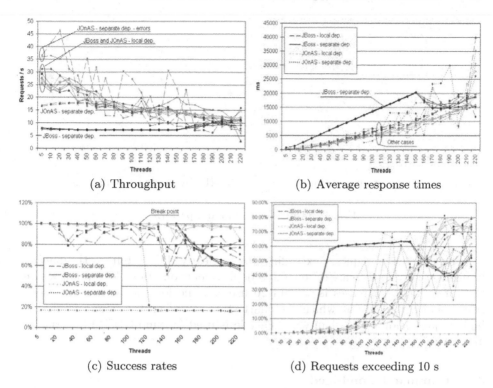

(a) Throughput

(b) Average response times

(c) Success rates

(d) Requests exceeding 10 s

Fig. 4. Results for Facade pattern

The number of requests with handling time exceeding 10 seconds differs clearly in the two different deployment cases. In the case of application layers deployed on one container, the number of late requests is not more than 10% until the break point is reached. In the case of application layers deployed separately on two containers, the late requests occur much earlier, at around 40 concurrent users, and the increase is very rapid. This is shown in Fig. 4(d).

4.2 Command

The character of throughput change for the application with Command pattern is very similar to that for the Facade implementation. Only in the case of JOnAS container is the throughput line flatter compared to the one for Facade. In general, the throughput value is lower than that of Facade. The difference between Command and Facade is shown in Fig. 3(a).

The average response time differs the most, when compared to Facade, in the case of separately deployed application on JBoss. The response time rises very steeply reaching 40 000 ms, while for Facade the peak was 20 000 ms (Figures 4(b) and 5(a)).

The characteristics of the success rate for Command are very similar to that for Facade. The rate for Command is a bit lower, though.

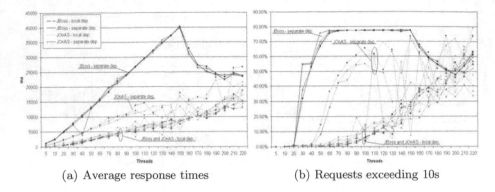

(a) Average response times　　　(b) Requests exceeding 10s

Fig. 5. Results for Command pattern

The number of requests exceeding 10s is clearly different from the Facade implementation in the case of separated deployments on JBoss. The point where the rate sharply increases is around 20 users, while for Facade it is 40 users. Additionally, the rate at which the chart stabilises when Command is used is higher (just below 80%) than when Facade is used (around 60%), Figures 4(d) and 5(b).

4.3　Command Combined

For the Command Combined, the throughput changes are very similar to those for Facade and Command. However, the throughput is clearly higher than the one for Command and lower than for Facade (Fig. 3(a)).

The average response time, again, has similar characteristic to previous cases, with the difference that the actual values are higher than for Facade and lower when compared to Command. For example, for a separately deployed application on JBoss, the peak of the average time is around 25 000 ms, while it is 20 000 ms and 40 000 ms for Facade and Command, respectively (Fig. 6).

The success rate for Command Combined implementation is very similar to that of Facade and Command implementations, but its value may again be between Facade and Command. However, the difference is not very clear in all the cases due to noise.

The rate of requests exceeding 10s tends to be similar to the one for Command implementation, Fig. 5(b). However, the point where the number rapidly increases is similar to the one for Facade implementation, Fig. 4(d). The results for Command Combined again are between Command and Facade results.

4.4　Results Summary

The differences between particular test cases can be explained at many levels. First, it can be the particular EJB container implementation, which influences values of the results. An example of this is the throughput achieved on JBoss and

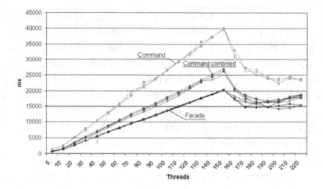

Fig. 6. Average response times in the case of separate deployments on JBoss

JOnAS containers. As the goal of the tests was not to compare the performance of EJB containers, but differences related to particular design patterns, the values are not relevant. What is important is that the scale of differences between the results for each pattern is corresponding for the different containers.

Second level can be the network traffic reduction and serialisation penalty. That could explain differences between implementations of design patterns deployed separately. For Facade, which had the best performance, serialisation was limited only to data value objects. Command, on the other hand, had the same number of network calls as Facade implementation, but additionally, it performed serialization of more complex objects, namely, objects consisting of the same data value objects and the Command itself. The compromise solution between Facade and Command, the Command Combined, had, on one hand, complex structure of objects to serialise, even more complex than Command (the data value objects and multiple commands). On the other hand, the overall number of calls was reduced, explaining its performance between Command and Facade.

There are also results that are not easy to throw light on. The noise, values that differed much between each test round within the same test case, are certainly not easy to explain. It can be noticed that locally deployed applications have higher tendency to produce ambiguous results. Taking a closer look at the results, it is possible to notice that values tend to lower just to increase almost to the previous level for the next number of simulated users. This happens, for example, in the cases of success rate. One explanation could be that the server could not handle the full number of requesting users and that resulted in the lower performance. However, consequently the container allocated more resources, for instance, bean and connection pools, and the next increased number of requests could be handled better.

5   Concluding Remarks

The tests carried out covered 12 different test cases with respect to implemented design pattern, EJB container, and deployment configuration. All the data gathered shows differences between the compared design patterns and consequences of their replacement, in terms of performance-related quality factors of the application. Regardless of the type of EJB container used and the way the application was deployed, the scale of differences remained nearly constant. In all the presented tests, the implementation that used Facade design pattern had the highest throughput. In addition, for each of the tested design patterns the characteristics of success rate and the number of requests exceeding 10 seconds were different. The number of users when the application stopped handling requests properly tends to be the highest also for Facade implementation.

Additionally, the presented differences between the variants of Command pattern indicate consequences of particular implementation choices. The Command Combined implementation reduced the number of network calls, which resulted in better performance than Command. Facade was clearly better than either of the Command variants, however.

Presented findings demonstrate significance of design decisions and their implications for multi-tier applications. The results can be utilised by application architects and designers to anticipate the behaviour of an application depending on chosen design solutions. An initial suggestion for designers indicates that for the local deployment scenario, which is unlikely in a production environment, there are no significant differences between Facade and Command patterns. At the same time, in the case of separately deployed presentation and business layers, which is a common deployment configuration, the differences between patterns point Facade as a better solution, from the performance point of view. However, if, for example, the service interface available for the client is required to be relatively simple (small number of methods), yet flexible (allowing easy extensions to the service), as mentioned in [10], then Command and especially Command Combined may be a more favourable choice than Facade.

The presented findings are a good starting point for further pattern comparisons. The results show differences between the selected design patterns. However, the conducted tests were limited to only two design patterns and a specific technology (J2EE). Therefore, extended tests should be conducted and cover multi-tier technologies different from the J2EE technology, for example .NET [18]. In addition, the tests should include a wider range of compared design patterns. The final aim would be a creation of a set of recommendations containing specific design patterns used on different layers of application and implemented in various technologies and variants.

Acknowledgements

I would like to thank Tarja Systä, from Tampere University of Technology, for her support during the tests and writing this paper. Additionally, I would like to thank Janne Mattila for presenting his tests results.

References

1. Erich Gamma, Richard Helm, Ralph Johnson, and John Vlissides. *Design patterns: elements of reusable object-oriented software*. Addison-Wesley, Boston, Massachusetts, 1995.
2. Serge Demeyer, Stephane Ducasse, and Oscar Nierstrasz. *Object-oriented Reengineering Patterns*. Elsevier Science, 2003.
3. Martin Fowler. *Analysis Patterns*. Addison-Wesley, 1997.
4. Sun Microsystems. Java 2 Enterprise Edition. http://java.sun.com/j2ee, 2004.
5. Emmanuel Cecchet, Julie Marguerite, and Willy Zwaenepoel. Performance and scalability of EJB applications. In *17th ACM Conference on ObjectOriented Programming*, pages 246–261, Seattle, Washington, 2002.
6. Paul Brebner and Jeffrey Gosper. How Scalable is J2EE Technology? In *ACM SIGSOFT Software Engineering News 28*, 2003.
7. Janne Mattila. EJB Performance. Master's thesis, Tampere University of Technology, 2004.
8. Yan Liu, Ian Gorton, Anna Liu, Ning Jiang, and Shiping Chen. Designing a test suite for empirically-based middleware performance prediction. In *The Fortieth International Confernece on Tools Pacific: Objects for internet, mobile and embedded applications*, Sydney, Australia, February 2002.
9. Giovanni Denaro, Andrea Polini, and Wolfgang Emmerich. Early performance testing of distributed software applications. In *ACM SIGSOFT Software Engineering Notes 29*, number 1, January 2004.
10. Floyd Marinescu. *EJB Design Patterns*. The MiddleWare Company, 2002.
11. Deepak Alur, John Crupi, and Dan Malks. *Core J2EE Patterns*. Sun Microsystems Press, 2001.
12. Apache. JMeter. http://jakarta.apache.org/jmeter/index.html, 2004.
13. JMeter Ant Task. http://www.programmerplanet.org/ant-jmeter, 2004.
14. JBoss EJB server. http://www.jboss.org, 2004.
15. JOnAS: Java Open Application Server. http://jonas.objectweb.org, 2004.
16. MySQL. http://www.mysql.com, 2004.
17. Apache Jakarta Tomcat. http://jakarta.apache.org/tomcat/index.html, 2004.
18. Microsoft Corporation. .NET. http://msdn.microsoft.com/netframework, 2004.

An MDA-Based Approach for Inferring Concurrency in Distributed Systems

Raul Silaghi and Alfred Strohmeier

Software Engineering Laboratory
Swiss Federal Institute of Technology in Lausanne
CH-1015 Lausanne EPFL, Switzerland
{Raul.Silaghi,Alfred.Strohmeier}@epfl.ch

Abstract. When dealing with distributed systems, one of the most important problems that has to be addressed is concurrency. Distributed systems are inherently concurrent, distributed objects being implicitly "shared" between all participating clients, and explicit concurrency control must be enforced if consistency is to be preserved. From an MDA perspective to software development, we show in this paper how concurrency resulting from distribution can be inferred in an automatic way, provided that a small set of design conventions are strictly adhered to. A simple PIM-level concurrency profile is considered in order to illustrate how the inference algorithm evolves on a concrete example and how an initial distributed design is automatically refined according to the proposed concurrency profile.

Keywords: Concurrency, Distributed Systems, Model-Driven Architecture, MDA, Model Transformations, Enterprise Fondue, UML Profiles.

1 Introduction

Software has become a driving technology. Embedded in systems of all kinds, ranging from transportation and medical systems to industrial and military applications while passing through office and entertainment products, software is virtually inescapable in a modern world, and people have accepted its omnipresence as a technological fact of life.

Over the last decade, there has been and still is an increasing need for integrating different (legacy) software systems and applications, which results in heterogeneous and often distributed systems. Moreover, the ever increasing popularity of the Internet and the growing field of e-commerce have led to an explosion of the number of distributed systems in operation. Such systems are typically required to provide highly available services, and must satisfy hundreds of clients *simultaneously*, raising the importance of middleware-specific concerns, such as *concurrency* and *transactions*, when designing distributed systems.

Model Driven Architecture (MDA) [1][2], the relatively new initiative launched by the Object Management Group (OMG), promotes a new approach to software development by clearly separating the "what" and the "how", or as stated in [2], "... that separates the specification of system functionality from the specification of the implementation of that functionality on a specific technology platform". Both specifications are expressed as models: *Platform Independent Models (PIMs)*, which specify the structure and functions of a system while abstracting away technical details, and *Platform Spe-*

N. Guelfi et al. (Eds.): FIDJI 2004, LNCS 3409, pp. 24–37, 2005.

cific Models (PSMs), which are derived from PIMs and specify how the functionality is to be realized on a selected platform. Since in this paper we consider the *middleware* to be our MDA platform, further on we will directly refer to the middleware instead of the general concept of (MDA) platform. Moreover, as the Unified Modeling Language (UML) [3] established itself as the de-facto industry standard, we only focus on the UML support for MDA.

Besides the obvious importance of PIMs and PSMs in MDA, *model transformations* are undoubtedly the key technology in the realization of the MDA vision [4]. Among other usages, model transformations are the ones responsible for refining PIMs into PSMs (or abstracting away from PSMs to PIMs) and mapping PSMs to concrete middleware-based implementations, providing thus an elegant approach to adapt PIMs to the peculiarities of the new middleware infrastructures that do not cease to appear.

From a pragmatic point of view, in order to be able to realize the code generation step of the MDA vision for distributed middleware-mediated systems, MDA needs to provide support for understanding, describing, and implementing different middleware-specific concerns, such as distribution, concurrency, transactions, security, and so on, also referred to as *pervasive services* in MDA's PIM terminology [2].

The MDA-compliant Enterprise Fondue [5] software development method defines MDA-oriented UML profiles that address middleware-specific concerns at different levels of abstraction. Enterprise Fondue also promotes a systematic approach to addressing pervasive services in an MDA-compliant manner, at different levels of abstraction, through incremental refinement steps along middleware-specific concern-dimensions according to the proposed UML profiles. A complete example has already been carried out for the distribution concern. The *UML-D Profiles* proposed in [6] address the distribution concern in an MDA-oriented fashion at three different levels of abstraction: *platform-independent* level, *abstract realization* level, and *concrete realization* level. The CORBA [7] technology was used in [6] to illustrate how the refinement process is applied to a concrete example.

Relying on the PIM-level outcome when refining along the distribution concern-dimension as presented in [6], we show in this paper how refining along the concurrency concern-dimension can be achieved in an automatic way, provided that a small set of design conventions are strictly adhered to. A simple PIM-level concurrency profile is considered in order to illustrate how the inference algorithm evolves on a concrete example and how an initial (distributed) design is automatically refined according to the proposed concurrency profile.

The rest of this paper is organized as follows: Section 2 provides the motivation of this work by pointing out the importance of concurrency in distributed systems and emphasizing the specific issues that are addressed later; Section 3 presents the inference algorithm along with a small set of design conventions on which it relies; Section 4 shows how the inference algorithm is applied to a concrete example, stressing the fuzzy and narrow border between concurrency and transactions, and Section 5 draws some conclusions and presents future work directions.

2   Motivation

From the very beginning we would like to stress that we will concentrate in this paper on concurrency as it occurs naturally in distributed systems, and neglect the specific problems related to concurrency in centralized systems or multiprocessor architectures. We will therefore present a systematic approach to assist the developer in addressing inherent concurrency in distributed systems.

In order to better illustrate the motivation behind this work, let's consider the object-oriented design of a simple Bank system, like the one presented in Figure 1, which has already been refined along the distribution concern-dimension at the PIM level of abstraction. We assume the example is enough self-explaining for not entering into more details. However, for more information about the distribution-related elements, please refer to [6] where we defined the entire hierarchy of UML-D Profiles at different MDA-levels of abstraction, together with MTL [8] model transformations that incrementally refine existing design models (within the same or between different MDA-levels) according to the proposed UML-D Profiles.

Typically, unless having a distributed system that provides its clients with constant values, such as mathematical or physical constants (π, e, c), distributed objects have

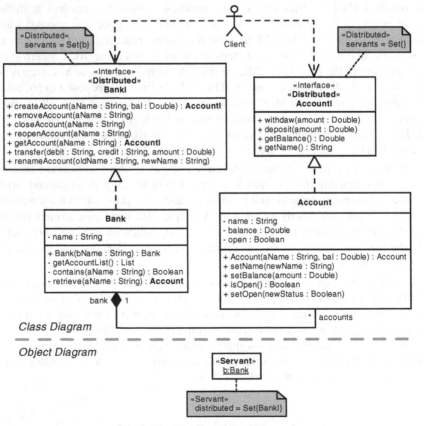

Fig. 1. The Distributed Bank Example

their own state, which is implicitly "shared" between all possible clients and therefore has to be protected from simultaneous accesses by concurrent clients if consistency is to be preserved. For instance, two clients concurrently accessing the Bank should not be allowed to transfer (transfer) money between accounts and to remove an account (removeAccount) at the same time since the very account that is removed might be one of the accounts participating in the transfer. Similarly, two clients concurrently accessing an Account should not deposit and withdraw at the same time, just like they should not withdraw and getBalance at the same time.

Some immediate questions arise. How can we detect such conflicts? Is it possible to automatically detect them without any previous knowledge about the semantics of those operations? And even if we detect such conflicting operations, and suppose we are relying on a *locking* mechanism for implementing concurrency control, how can we decide the right lock modes for those operations in order to preserve consistency but without a significant performance loss? Besides the obvious concurrency at the level of distributed operations (i.e., operations belonging to a «Distributed» interface), does distribution induce concurrent behavior at other levels of the system under development?

3   Inferring Concurrency Locks for Distributed Operations and Beyond

After a brief introduction of some concurrency concepts, we present in this section how refining along the concurrency concern-dimension (concurrency strictly induced by the «Distributed» interfaces) can be achieved in an automatic way, provided that a small set of design conventions are strictly adhered to. A simple concurrency profile is also proposed in order to support the inference algorithm at the PIM level of abstraction.

Many researchers view all object-oriented systems as inherently concurrent, since objects themselves are "naturally concurrent" entities. In sequential object-oriented programs, only one object is executing one of its methods at a given time. In concurrent object-oriented programs, several objects can be active at a given time, and even a given method might be invoked multiple times concurrently. Objects must be aware of this concurrency in order to guarantee state consistency in the presence of simultaneous method invocations.

The most common technique for implementing concurrency control is locking. A *lock* represents the ability of a specific client to access a specific resource, in our case a distributed object, in a particular way defined by the corresponding *lock mode*. Coordination is achieved by preventing multiple clients from simultaneously possessing locks for the same resource if the activities of those clients might conflict. A client must first acquire an appropriate lock before accessing a shared resource. Having a variety of lock modes allows for more flexible conflict resolution. For example, providing different modes for reading and writing allows a resource to support multiple concurrent "readers", i.e., clients that are only reading the state of the resource, improving in this way the performance of the final system.

Based on these very few concepts, we defined a simple concurrency profile like the one shown in Figure 2. Ignoring any low level implementation details, the profile defines a single stereotype called «Locked» as an extension of the Operation metaclass

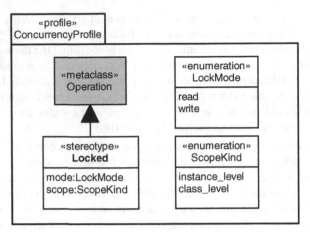

Fig. 2. Simplified View of the Concurrency Profile at PIM Level

specifying whether an operation should be locked or not. Two tag definitions define the lock mode (`mode`), either `read` or `write`, and the scope of locking (`scope`), either at the instance level (`instance_level`) or at the class level (`class_level`) depending on whether the operation accesses object-specific properties or class-specific properties (e.g., `static` fields in Java). Please note that the proposed profile is not at all complete, Figure 2 showing only the part that is relevant for this paper.

Since it might not be very clear from the definition of the profile, we would like to point out now that locks are indeed acquired at object/resource level *but* the code that must trigger the acquisition of such locks must be generated at class level, more precisely inside the operations that access (read/write) the state of the potential objects instance of that class. By specifying which operations should be locked, we will later on know where the appropriate concurrency control code must be generated.

Following the Enterprise Fondue principles, this PIM-level concurrency profile could be further refined into a CORBA Concurrency Control Service (CCS) [9] profile at the PSM level of abstraction. Such a refinement step should enhance the PIM-level profile with new locking modes supported by the CORBA CCS, and should make a clear distinction between locks that have been acquired on behalf of the current thread and those acquired on behalf of a transaction, another specificity of the CORBA CCS. At code level, we would rely on a concrete implementation of the CORBA CCS by an ORB vendor, such as the one provided by OpenORB [10].

We discuss now in more details the implementation of the MTL model transformation that automatically refines a distributed design along the concurrency concern-dimension at the PIM level of abstraction according to the concurrency profile proposed in Figure 2.

3.1   JavaBeans-Like Design Conventions

Before applying the inference algorithm, the developer must ensure that the input model conforms to a small set of JavaBeans-like [11] design conventions.

First of all, we define so called *primitive* operations as those that access the state of distributed objects and cannot be further broken into smaller units. A JavaBeans-like design convention associates with each such primitive operation a lock mode that it promotes at the level of its usage. The list of primitive operations, and their lock modes, contains:

- `get*`, getters, retrieve the values of the attributes that are part of an object's state; [mode = read];
- `set*`, setters, modify the values of the attributes that are part of an object's state; [mode = write];
- `is*`, getters, retrieve the values of the boolean attributes that are part of an object's state; [mode = read];
- `insert`, for inserting a new item in a multiobject, e.g., inserting a new `Element` in a `List`; [mode = write];
- `remove`, for removing an item from a multiobject, e.g., removing an `Element` from a `List`; [mode = write];
- `iterate`, for traversing through a multiobject's items, e.g., traversing the `Elements` in a `List`, one `Element` at a time; [mode = read];

For instance, a non-primitive operation using two getters, one setter, and an iterator, all acting on the same "self" object, should lock itself in the strongest lock mode promoted by one of the primitive operations it encapsulates. In this concrete example, it is the setter that dictates the `write` lock mode.

Second, taking into account that the entire inference algorithm inspects collaboration/sequence diagrams, these diagrams must be prepared with extreme care by the developer in order for the automatic model transformation to be successful. If necessary, collaboration/sequence diagrams should be refactored in order to ensure that all operations are explicitly called and that a JavaBeans-style is strictly adhered to, i.e., the state of an object should only be accessed/modified through explicit calls of the corresponding getter/setter operations. Figure 3 shows how such a refactoring looks like. For readability and lack of space reasons, we use Java code snippets instead of showing collaboration/sequence diagrams.

Finally, the last convention is nothing else but stressing the fact that a multiobject is an intrinsic property of the "container" object. For instance, the list of accounts is an intrinsic property of the `Bank` object. Any `insert` or `remove` operation performed on the multiobject changes its state, and thus changes the state of the `Bank`. As we will see later, this strong hypothesis could be released by considering concurrency control at a finer granularity level, e.g., at the object attribute level.

3.2 The Inference Algorithm

The main goal of the inference algorithm is to automatically apply the PIM-level concurrency profile proposed in Figure 2 to all possible concurrent operations. Implement-

```
void Account::deposit(amount:double) {          void Account::deposit(amount:double) {
    balance += amount;                              double d = this.getBalance();
}                                                   d += amount;
                                                    this.setBalance(d);
                                                }
```

a. Original Code	b. Refactored Code

Fig. 3. Refactoring Collaboration/Sequence Diagrams

ed as an MTL model transformation, the inference algorithm is applied at model level, relying entirely on the interactions described in collaboration/sequence diagrams.

Since we are analyzing only the concurrency resulting from distribution, the inference algorithm starts by looking at the collaboration/sequence diagrams of all distributed operations that appear in the distributed design that the model transformation takes as input. Please notice that by *distributed operation* we intend any operation that belongs to a «Distributed» interface, as defined in [6].

For each distributed operation, depending on the interactions it defines in its associated collaboration/sequence diagram, and based on the conventions defined in section 3.1, the algorithm determines and assigns the most appropriate lock mode that would protect the state of the distributed object in case other (or the same) distributed operations are invoked concurrently. Figure 4 shows an example where two distributed operations, distributedOp_A and distributedOp_B, are called on two different distributed objects, aInstance and bInstance, each such object being associated with its own lock, lockA and lockB. The question is what lock modes (r/w) should be associated with the two distributed operations, i.e., in what lock mode (r/w) should those operations lock the target objects in order to preserve their consistency?

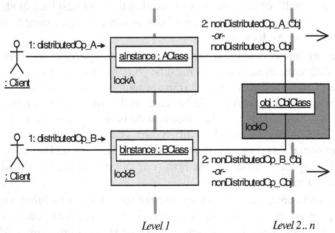

Level 1   *Level 2..n*

Fig. 4. "Distributed" Concurrent Operations at Different Levels

Setting the lock lockA on the object aInstance when the distributed operation distributedOp_A is called will only protect the distributed object aInstance from other distributed, and potentially concurrent, operations invoked on the same object. However, as illustrated in Figure 4, there might be other operation calls inside a distributed operation that crosscut the boundaries of the distributed object. For instance, from within the distributed operation distributedOp_A, the non-distributed operation nonDistributedOp_A_Obj is invoked on an object obj, which is not protected by any locks. If lockA is set in read mode, or if it is not set at all (the object aInstance does not have any state to protect), all concurrent calls to distributedOp_A will pass through the aInstance object, will concurrently arrive at the object obj, and thus the consistency of its state cannot be guaranteed. Similarly, if lockA is set in write mode, it will block all incoming concurrent calls at the level of aInstance. As a consequence, by way of aInstance, there will be only one client calling the operation nonDistributedOp_A_Obj at a given time. However, as shown in Figure 4, it is enough to have another distributed object bInstance, with lockB set in write mode as well, to cause the same concurrency problems as before at the level of the object obj, i.e., two concurrent clients, entering through the aInstance and bInstance respectively, will simultaneously call the operations nonDistributedOp_A_Obj and nonDistributedOp_B_Obj on the object obj, and thus the consistency of its state cannot be guaranteed. One should notice that nonDistributedOp_A_Obj and nonDistributedOp_B_Obj do not necessarily have to be different operations, as we tried to illustrate in Figure 4. Even if both objects aInstance and bInstance call the same nonDistributedOp_Obj operation on the object obj, the consistency of its state cannot be guaranteed.

The two locks, lockA and lockB, ensure consistency but only at the level where they are defined, in this case the first level, also referred to as the front-end of a system. However, as showed in the example above, the concurrency induced by distribution is not always limited to the front-end. Instead it propagates to the following levels as well.

The inference algorithm that we propose takes care of these problems as well, tracing each operation down to its primitive operations and defining (stronger) locks at the highest possible levels, i.e., as far as possible from the front-end. In fact, in order to easily handle the concurrency induced by distribution at any level, the inference algorithm is recursive. Once the potential "distributed" concurrent operations are identified, such as nonDistributedOp_A_Obj and nonDistributedOp_B_Obj, the algorithm is recursively invoked to address these operations and to determine the most appropriate lock modes for them as well.

The inference algorithm could be summarized as follows:

- iterate over all distributed operations, i.e., over all operations defined in «Distributed» interfaces;
- for each distributed operation perform an in-depth analysis of its corresponding collaboration/sequence diagram;
- if the distributed operation is also a primitive operation, then use its own promoted lock to define the lock mode for the distributed operation;
- if the distributed operation is a non-primitive operation, then break it down into primitive operations and construct two different sets of operations: the Inner set and the Outer set;
- the Inner set will contain all primitive operations acting on the current object (e.g., this in Java), i.e., on the object on which the distributed operation under consideration is defined; the strongest lock mode promoted by all primitive operations in the Inner set will determine the lock mode to be set for the distributed operation under consideration;
- the Outer set will contain all operations (primitive or not) that are not acting on the current object; every time such an operation is encountered, the operation will simply be placed in the Outer set without breaking it further down into primitive operations;

- for all the classes of the operations in the Outer sets, compute a union of all their operations that appear throughout the Outer sets, i.e., all the operations that appear in at least one Outer set; as a consequence, for each class we will obtain an Inferred set containing all operations belonging to that class that have been called from distributed operations;
- iterate over all Inferred sets;
- if the cardinality of an Inferred set is greater than one, then run recursively the algorithm for all the operations in the Inferred set;
- if the cardinality of an Inferred set is one, then check whether the operation in the Inferred set belongs to more than one Outer set (the cardinality might be one because of the union operation, but the operation might belong to several Outer sets, {op}∪{op}={op}); if this is the case, then run recursively the algorithm for the operation in the Inferred set; this is necessary in order to address the special case, already presented when discussing Figure 4, when two objects aInstance and bInstance may call the same nonDistributedOp_Obj operation on the object obj from two different distributed operations;
- if the cardinality of an Inferred set is one, and the operation in the Inferred set belongs to exactly one Outer set, then check the lock mode that was set for the distributed operation from where the operation in the Inferred set was called; there are two cases now: (i) if the lock is set in write mode, then no lock mode needs to be set for the operation in the Inferred set, and (ii) if the lock is set in read mode, then run recursively the algorithm for the operation in the Inferred set; these two cases were explained on the example discussed in Figure 4 when we showed how the lock mode associated with the operation distributedOp_A of the object aInstance had an impact on the consistency of the state of object obj.

One should notice that, on one hand, Inner and Outer sets are built for each *collaboration/sequence diagram* of a distributed operation, or of a potential "distributed" concurrent operation that has been identified by the inference algorithm, and they classify the operations (Class::Operation) that appear in such collaboration/sequence diagrams into two disjoint subsets. On the other hand, Inferred sets are built for each *class* and they contain all the operations belonging to that class that appear in at least one Outer set at a given step in the recursive application of the inference algorithm.

4   Applying the Inference Algorithm to a Concrete Case Study

After having described the algorithm in the previous section, we present here a trace of applying it to a concrete case study, namely the Bank system introduced in section 2.

The simplest case in assigning lock modes is when the distributed operation is also primitive, as is the case of Account::getBalance and Account::getName, which will both get assigned a read lock mode, corresponding to the lock modes they promote.

If we consider the Account::deposit operation, as shown in Figure 5, one can easily notice that the Outer set is empty, while the Inner set contains two primitive operations, namely Account::getBalance and Account::setBalance. Based on the lock modes promoted by these two primitive operations, the lock mode for Ac-

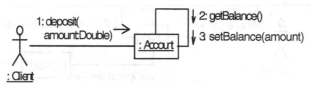

Fig. 5. `Account::deposit`

`count::deposit` is set to the strongest between the two, i.e., a `write` mode is set. The `Account::withdraw` operation follows the same reasoning and gets assigned a `write` mode as well.

The `Bank::transfer` operation, illustrated in Figure 6, is more complex than the previous ones and enters more deeply in the details of the inference algorithm. For instance, the `Bank::retrieve` operation needs to be further broken down into primitive operations, resulting in an `Inner` set containing {`Bank::getAccountList, Bank::iterate`}, and an `Outer` set containing {`Account::getName, Account::isOpen, Account::withdraw, Account::deposit`}. One should notice that the `Bank` is used inside the `Inner` set also for operations that pertain to the list of accounts. This is because of the last convention introduced in section 3.1, which defines the list of accounts (a multiobject) to be an intrinsic property of the `Bank` (its "container" object). Analyzing the `Inner` set, the inference algorithm assigns a `read` lock mode for the `Bank::transfer` operation, since at the level of the `Bank` we are only reading and traversing the list of accounts. Looking at the `Outer` set, the `Inferred` set is easy to construct since all operations belong to the same class, namely `Account`. As a consequence, there will be only one `Inferred` set containing all four operations. The algorithm is then recursively applied to resolve the lock modes for these operations. One can notice that three of the operations are in fact distributed operations and they would have been assigned a lock mode anyway. However, this is not the case for the `Account::isOpen`, which seems to induce concurrency even though not in the initial list of distributed operations. This is a typical example where the concurrency induced by distributed operations crosscuts the border of the front-end distributed objects and propagates to other objects in the system (in this particular case, the `Account` objects are also distributed, but it might not have been the case). The recursive application of the inference algorithm will assign a lock mode for the `Account::isOpen` operation, which is a rather straight forward job considering that it deals with a primitive operation as well.

Without entering into too many details this time, the inference algorithm continues to analyze the collaboration/sequence diagrams of all distributed operations inferring as

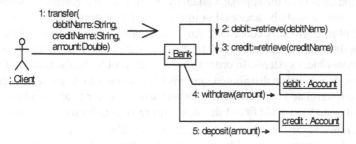

Fig. 6. `Bank::transfer`

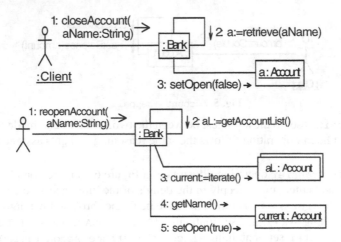

Fig. 7. `Bank::closeAccount` and `Bank::reopenAccount`

many concurrent operations as possible and assigning appropriate locks for each such operation. For instance, analyzing the `Bank::closeAccount` or `Bank::reopenAccount` operations, both shown in Figure 7, the algorithm will infer that the operation `Account::setOpen` should have its own lock as well, and will recursively analyze what would be the most appropriate lock mode to assign for it.

If we were to state the main benefit of our inference algorithm, we would say that it manages to discover all possible concurrency "*entry points*" in a distributed system and locks them appropriately in order to ensure the consistency in the presence of concurrent access to distributed objects. However, because of the *automatic* inference and because we detect and lock *all potential* concurrent operations, the performance of the final system might be significantly diminished while the risk to consistency is decreased as well. In order to balance these two factors, namely the level of concurrency and the risk to consistency, developers may loose the locks inferred by our algorithm according to the actual semantics of the application under development.

4.1   The Transactions' Border

However, distributed concurrent systems often give rise to complex concurrent and interacting activities. Such systems often need more advanced and elaborate concurrency features which may go beyond the traditional concurrency control associated with separate operation calls (like the approach taken by our inference algorithm). Because multiple objects must usually be accessed or updated *together*, great care must be taken to keep related objects globally consistent. Any interruption when updating objects, or interleaving updates and accesses to objects, can break the overall consistency of distributed concurrent object systems. In order to solve such problems, the notion of *transaction* has been introduced in distributed systems [12]. Transactions must be used to correctly handle interrelated and concurrent updates to objects (or to any kind of data to be more general), and to provide fault tolerance with respect to hardware failures.

The inference algorithm presented in section 3.2 addresses the concurrency control in a completely automatic way, without any previous knowledge about the semantics of the operations involved. However, this version of the inference algorithm does not go beyond the traditional concurrency control associated with separate operation calls.

Let's consider the example of the `Bank::renameAccount` operation in order to illustrate the current limitations of the algorithm. Figure 8 presents the collaboration diagram for the operation, pseudocode showing how the operation breaks down into primitive operations, and the different sets that are constructed during the inference algorithm. Once the inference finishes, the `Bank::renameAccount` operation will get assigned a read lock mode, the `Account::getName` a read lock mode, the `Account::isOpen` a read lock mode, and finally the `Account::setName` a write lock mode. One may notice how locks are associated with separate operations. Suppose now that two clients issue the following two calls simultaneously:

- [client 1] `Bank.renameAccount("Matrix", "Revolutions");`
- [client 2] `Bank.renameAccount("Reloaded", "Revolutions");`

Due to the read lock at the level of the `Bank`, and several read locks at the level of the `Accounts`, both calls can be executed concurrently. Even the two `Account::setName` operations will be executed concurrently because they involve two different objects. However, after the execution, the list of accounts will contain two different accounts with the same name, i.e., "`Revolutions`", which breaks the overall consistency of the Bank system. The reason is that between the moment when we check whether the new name is already used by another account in the list (`contains(newName)`), and the moment when we actually set the new name for the account under consideration (`setName(newName)`), many other concurrent activities may occur, such as another `renameAccount` operation, like in this example.

As described in the very beginning of this section, this is a typical example of interleaving updates and accesses to objects, which should also be addressed in order to guarantee the consistency of the overall system. Even though we do not support this level of concurrency control, the current inference algorithm could be enhanced to signal such dependencies within an operation. Indeed, if we have a closer look at the `Outer`

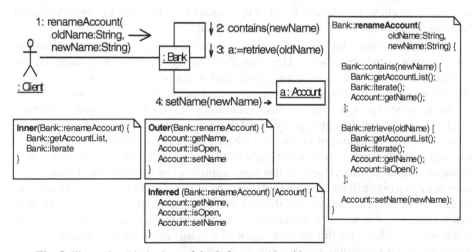

Fig. 8. Illustrating Limitations of the Inference Algorithm (`Bank::renameAccount`)

set in Figure 8, one can easily see that there are both readers and writers on the Account, e.g., getName, isOpen, setName, which could trigger a signal that some more advanced and elaborate concurrency control mechanisms might be needed. In such situations, the most elegant solution would be to group together the critical operations in a transaction, and rely on the ACID properties [12] of transactions to guarantee the overall consistency of the system. In fact, at implementation level, the CORBA Concurrency Control Service [9] allows the developer to acquire locks on behalf of the current thread or on behalf of a transaction, which is exactly what is needed. However, for the time being, we believe that the semantics of operations must be known to the application developer if transactional features are to be integrated, which is not the case for concurrency control. As we showed with our inference algorithm, concurrency control may be automatically inferred, enforcing consistency constraints up to a certain level, up to what we call the transactions' border.

5   Conclusions and Future Work

The omnipresence of distributed systems nowadays, with multiple clients simultaneously accessing distributed resources, puts a high emphasis on the design and implementation of concurrency control as a means to ensure consistency in distributed systems. Adopting an MDA approach to software development, we showed in this paper how the concurrency induced by distribution can be inferred in an automatic way, provided that a small set of JavaBeans-like design conventions are strictly adhered to. A simple PIM-level concurrency profile was considered in order to illustrate how the inference algorithm evolves on a concrete example and how an initial distributed design is automatically refined according to the proposed concurrency profile.

The fuzzy and narrow border between concurrency and transactions was discussed as well. The current inference algorithm is able to automatically detect concurrent operations, without any previous knowledge about their semantics, and assign them appropriate lock modes in order to preserve consistency. Even though the same algorithm could be easily enhanced to point out operations where transactional features might be required, we believe that the semantics of operations must be known to the application developer if transactional features are to be integrated.

In the current state, there is only one lock per object managing the whole concurrency control at the object level. However, this has significant consequences on the overall performance of the system in general, and on the degree of concurrency that an object may support in particular. In order to overcome this limitation, we would like to define the concurrency control at a finer granularity level, e.g., at the object attribute level, just as it is already supported by the CORBA Concurrency Control Service at implementation level. Instead of locking the whole object, we would use dedicated locks for each attribute that is part of the object's state, along with a system of dependencies between attributes, if necessary. In this way, simultaneous invocations of two operations acting on two different attributes of the same object, e.g., Account::setName and Account::getBalance, would be allowed to execute concurrently. We also believe that the analysis that has to be performed in order to infer such finer granularity locks could serve as a basis for further investigations towards automatically inferring transactional features in distributed concurrent systems.

References

[1]   Object Management Group, Inc.: *Model Driven Architecture*. http://www.omg.org/mda/ November 2004.

[2]   Miller, J.; Mukerji, J.: *Model Driven Architecture (MDA)*. Object Management Group, Document ormsc/2001-07-01, July 2001.

[3]   Object Management Group, Inc.: *Unified Modeling Language Superstructure Specification*, v2.0, August 2003.

[4]   Sendall, S.; Kozaczynski, W.: *Model Transformation – the Heart and Soul of Model-Driven Software Development*. IEEE Software, **20**(5), Special Issue on Model-Driven Development, 2003, pp. 42 – 45. An extended version is available as Technical Report, EPFL-IC-LGL N° IC/2003/52, July 2003.

[5]   Silaghi, R.; Strohmeier, A.: *Integrating CBSE, SoC, MDA, and AOP in a Software Development Method*. Proceedings of the 7th IEEE International Enterprise Distributed Object Computing Conference, EDOC, Brisbane, Queensland, Australia, September 16-19, 2003. IEEE Computer Society, 2003, pp. 136 – 146. Also available as Technical Report, N° IC/2003/57, Swiss Federal Institute of Technology in Lausanne, Switzerland, September 2003.

[6]   Silaghi, R.; Fondement, F.; Strohmeier, A.: *Towards an MDA-Oriented UML Profile for Distribution*. Proceedings of the 8th IEEE International Enterprise Distributed Object Computing Conference, EDOC, Monterey, CA, USA, September 20-24, 2004. IEEE Computer Society, 2004, pp. 227 – 239. Also available as Technical Report, N° IC/2004/49, Swiss Federal Institute of Technology in Lausanne, Switzerland, May 2004.

[7]   Object Management Group, Inc.: *Common Object Request Broker Architecture: Core Specification*, v3.0.3, March 2004.

[8]   French National Institute for Research in Computer Science and Control (INRIA): *Model Transformation Language (MTL)*. http://modelware.inria.fr/, November 2004.

[9]   Object Management Group, Inc.: *Concurrency Control Service Specification*, v1.0, April 2000.

[10]   The Community OpenORB Project: *OpenORB*. http://openorb.sourceforge.net/, November 2004.

[11]   Sun Microsystems, Inc.: *JavaBeans Specification*, v1.01, August 1997.

[12]   Gray, J.; Reuter, A.: *Transaction Processing: Concepts and Techniques*. Morgan Kaufmann Publishers, 1993.

[13]   Bernstein, P. A.; Hadzilacos, V.; Goodman, N.: *Concurrency Control and Recovery in Database Systems*. Addison-Wesley, 1987.

[14]   Bernstein, P. A.; Goodman, N.: *Concurrency Control in Distributed Database Systems*. ACM Computing Surveys, **13**(2), June 1981, pp. 185 – 221.

[15]   Briot, J.-P.; Guerraoui, R.; Lohr, K.-P.: *Concurrency and Distribution in Object-Oriented Programming*. ACM Computing Surveys, **30**(3), September 1998, pp. 291 – 329.

[16]   Tripathi, A.; Oosten, J. V.; Miller, R.; *Object-Oriented Concurrent Programming Languages and Systems*. Journal of Object-Oriented Programming, **12**(7), November/December 1999, pp. 22 – 29.

[17]   Elmagarmid, A. K.: *Database Transaction Models for Advanced Applications*. Morgan Kaufmann Publishers, 1992.

[18]   Weikum, G.; Vossen, G.: *Transactional Information Systems: Theory, Algorithms, and the Practice of Concurrency Control and Recovery*. Morgan Kaufmann Publishers, 2001.

[19]   Hoare, C. A. R.: *Monitors: An Operating Systems Structuring Concept*. Communications of the ACM, **17**(10), October 1974, pp. 549 – 557.

Task-Based Access Control for Virtual Organizations

Panos Periorellis and Savas Parastatidis

School of Computing Science, University of Newcastle
Newcastle upon Tyne, NE1 7RU, UK
{Panayiotis.Periorellis,Savas.Parastatidis}@newcastle.ac.uk

Abstract. GOLD (Grid-based Information Models to Support the Rapid Innovation of New High Value-Added Chemicals) is concerned with the dynamic formation and management of virtual organisations in order to exploit market opportunities. The project aims to deliver the enabling technology to support the creation, operation and successful dissolution of such virtual organisations. A set of middleware technologies are designed and being implemented to address issues such as trust, security, contract management and monitoring, information management, etc. for virtual collaboration between companies. In this paper we discuss the set of requirements for access control in dynamic virtual organisations that have been defined as part of the trust-related work. We propose a solution, which extends the ideas of role based access control (RBAC), and we examine the use of existing and emerging Web Services technologies as an implementation platform.

1 Introduction

The GOLD project aims to build the infrastructure that enables organisations to collaborate securely in order to achieve some common goal, enabling the formation of virtual organisations (VOs). The project deals with a number of concepts such as roles, permissions, obligations within an environment comprised largely of autonomous components which are brought together to form a VO. Part of the requirements state that interactions between components are done dynamically without any prior collaboration history. This has an obvious impact of the amount of trust participants[1] in the VO can place on each other. Our aim is to alleviate this problem (i.e. establish trust without historical information) by enhancing certain security aspects of our system. Within GOLD, we are tackling trust issues in 3 distinct ways:

- We are implementing access control policies that will protect each party's assets from unauthorized use while allowing sharing;
- We are working on issues relating to dependable systems architecture as a way of enhancing trust through system trustworthiness [1]; and

---

[1] In this paper, the terms "party" and "participants" refer to those autonomous components that form part of the system and collaborate/interact using the GOLD infrastructure.

N. Guelfi et al. (Eds.): FIDJI 2004, LNCS 3409, pp. 38–47, 2005.

- We are investigating the formation of trust zones[2] by developing rules to which all participants of the system adhere.

In this paper we are looking into access control requirements for dynamic systems such as virtual organizations. The paper is organised as follows. First we take a look at trust in general and discuss access control and the current state of the art. We discuss the general access control requirements and propose a solution which draws from previous experience and past projects the authors have been involved in. We conclude with a discussion on the current state of the art of the Web Services technologies that can be used to provide such a solution.

2 Trust

Trust is a non-functional system property. It emerges through sound structure, security and dependability. In computing literature the meaning of trust has shifted from a purely non-functional property, related directly to dependability [1], to a measurement of the accuracy of access control models and contract management. In the course of this paper we will address both structuring issues as well as functional aspects.

Trust is based mainly on information (how much you know about someone), history (past transactional experiences with someone), or context (being within a trust zone or a boundary of rules and regulations with someone). In all the above cases trust can be a direct evaluation between 2 parties such that *a* trusts *b*. In highly dynamic environments such as virtual organisations parties may not have the opportunity to create a history of transactions. Additionally, there is also a requirement to maintain one's privacy which gives rise to identity issues. Since historical data and identity can be compromised, the only visible avenues towards achieving some degree of trust between two collaborative parties are *third parties* and *value*. Value and the wider notion of added value (although out of the scope of this work) is a motivating factor when trust related information is missing. In the virtual world and in particular in virtual collaborations that require anonymity, privacy and they lack any historical context, the only visible avenue for achieving some degree of trust is the transfer of trust from the collaborating parties, to the medium via which they collaborate. In our case this medium is the infrastructure which we hope to provide in GOLD. It is the infrastructure that provides guarantees to each party involved in a collaboration, that their *trust policies* will be enforced while at the same time maintaining identity and identity related information private. Trust policies, which are the focus of this discussion, are essentially security policies which express a party's requirements to engage into a transaction or any form of collaboration with any other

---

[2] The term refers to a conceptual boundary around all the components of the system. Components within a trust zone have agreed on certain rules and regulations prior to offering any services.

party. A party for example may require that data is exchanged encrypted using a specific encryption algorithm.

Policies can be dynamic and altered to reflect new security requirements. This generates the need for an environment with dynamic activation and de-activation of access control rights, and a move from a *passive security* policy, where permissions are assigned to particular roles, to an *active security* policy that distinguishes between roles and their instances.

3 Access Control

Active Control Lists (ACLs) have already been proven to be inefficient [2, 3]. Access lists built for every user lead to repetition of lists for users with similar rights. An extension to the ACL model is Role Based Access Control (RBAC) [4], which provides an additional security layer between the user and the resource. Access rights are given to roles (usually pre-determined) and then users are associated with those roles. The role-based access control model is more efficient since users are assigned roles rather that access lists. This implies that users of similar access rights are assigned a single role (i.e. a single ACL is assigned to many users), making the roles based approach a lot faster.

There are cases however when role-based access is also insufficient and, hence, additional security layers are required. Roshan [5] pointed out an example with a hospital emergency room, which demonstrates the problem. He explained that within an emergency room, *patients* and *doctors* are two typical roles. *Diagnosis* and *prescription* are rights of the *doctor* and therefore *doctors* need to have permissions to access *patient*'s details. This however does not imply that *doctors* are permitted to prescribe to any *patient*. Only assigned *doctors* have access rights and consequently permission to prescribe to a particular *patient*. In other words, there is a binding between a *doctor* role instance with the *patient* role instance, which implies the need for an additional layer that binds instances of roles with instances of resources. We therefore need a more dynamic access management system than RBAC.

GOLD requires similar bindings since we want to be able to restrict role access on resources depending on the execution context. In a virtual organisation the execution context can be regarded as the particular project or the goal that all participants have come together to achieve. In a virtual organisation there can be many projects with various participants resulting to complicated interrelationships between them. For example, some of them may play the same role in various projects, carrying out the exact same tasks, or have different roles within the same project depending on the performed task.

The question we raise is 'Should a role have the same permission and access rights throughout the set of similar or even identical projects and the tasks within those projects?' Our view is that in dynamic access control systems we should separate roles from role instances. Different role instances may require different permissions and indeed additional levels of authorisation depending on the project and task in which they are active.

The main GOLD case study involves the collaboration of a number of participants to enable the development of chemicals. The domain itself requires the sharing of sensitive information between participants who may have conflicting interests. In order to raise the levels of trust within such a VO we need to make sure that we have developed fine grained access control mechanisms. RBAC or other traditional techniques do not provide this level of granularity.

The main issues regarding access control relate to the degree of granularity embedded in the controlling mechanism itself. By granularity we refer to the level of detail for which we are prepared to define access rights. In GOLD, the simple subject-object permissions model on which RBAC is based is not sufficient. We need fine grained permissions for instances of roles as well as instances of objects. For example, a chemist role may be granted access to chemical documents but we do not however wish to grant access to all chemical documents produced by the system. Instead, we want any access permissions granted to the chemist role to be project-specific (e.g., the instance of a particular collaboration) as well as task-specific (e.g., the instance of a particular pre-defined activity). The management of roles and access permissions in GOLD is integrated with the management and monitoring of dynamic service level agreement or contracts between the participating services. The contracts can capture the expectations from specific tasks, using pre- and post-conditions. Permissions for roles can be activated and de-activated based on the progress of the monitored contracts.

4 Our Approach

4.1 Requirements

We need to develop a framework that defines conceptual boundaries around projects and tasks so that the roles and permissions can be scoped. Since a VO is comprised from a set of services, messages between those services need to propagate context-related information that can be used to identify the specific scope in which the security-related decisions can be made. Services can use the context information to determine whether the requestor has sufficient permission to perform operations or access resources. Other levels of requestor verification, such as authentication, could be implemented using existing methodologies (e.g., certificate-based authentication) and RBAC using access lists associated with every role.

The framework must allow for the dynamic activation and deactivation of permissions and roles based on progress monitoring of projects and tasks based on established contracts. For example, if a role fails to deliver its obligations within a task, we may want to de-activate certain permissions to that role. Also, if a task is completed successfully, we may want to add more permissions to a particular role so that resources and actions in a following task become accessible. In essence, the effective permissions are linked with the scope of the activity being performed.

4.2 Solution

The solution we propose follows the same model as previous works in handling transactions in distributed systems [6], the concept of spheres of control [7], and the coordinated atomic actions concept [8]. Coordinated Atomic (CA) Actions is a unified scheme for coordinating complex concurrent activities and supporting error recovery between multiple interacting components in distributed systems. CA Actions can be regarded as providing some of the generality of spheres of control and within them they offer a full support for maintaining consistency and achieving fault tolerance. They have been successfully applied [6, 9] as a structuring mechanism and they are relevant because they allow us to design, structure and provide fault tolerance in GOLD where autonomous organisational entities co-operate. We distinguish between role instances, resource instances as well as the notions of projects and tasks (. We are implementing the conceptual elements of this solution using WS standards. We discuss these in section 6.

5 Project-Task Structure

In order to achieve the level of granularity mentioned earlier we need to provide several levels of access control enforcement. In the first instance these manifest themselves as boundaries; that is project and task boundaries. The task boundary encapsulates all roles and objects related to an atomic action or activity. A project boundary encapsulates all tasks – atomic and otherwise – that take place within a GOLD VO in order to achieve a common goal. The concept of task is an implementation of the concept of spheres of control and is employed to provide a conceptual boundary encapsulating a specific action. Within its boundaries we find the following:

- a task name, i.e. unique identifier of a particular instance of a task;
- a set of roles;
- objects/resources used by that task; and
- reference(s) to resource(s) relevant to the task outside the tasks boundary.
- Pre-conditions, Post-conditions.

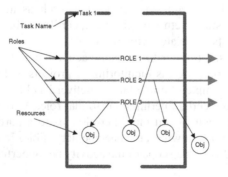

Fig. 1. The structure of a task

Figure 1 provides a conceptual representation of a task within GOLD. The box denotes the boundaries of the task within which the instances of roles and the set of access permissions are active. This logical task can span across multiple GOLD services. Each of the resources/objects in Figure 1 is associated with access permissions. The system evaluates access to the resources according to the role that attempts to perform an action always within the context of a particular task.

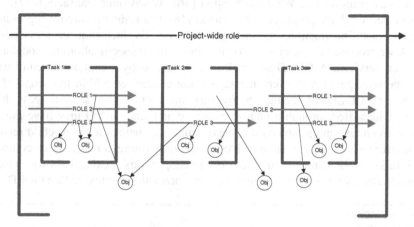

Fig. 2. Project structure

The Figure 2 illustrates the relationship between projects, tasks, role instances, and the objects/resources. In the context of GOLD, the project would be a VO that is established for the development and market exploitation of a chemical compound while a task could be a chemical hazard analysis. Objects that are shared between tasks (as project-bound objects) can be VO-wide documents while task-bound objects can be temporary notes used for the completion of that task. Roles may evolve according to the contracts put in place to manage the VO. For example, an employee from one company with an assigned role L may have access to some of the documents from another company during task B but will be denied access to them during the preceding task A. The contracts that are in place to establish a VO determine the roles and their permissions for each of the task that VO is to perform. The runtime support for the VO monitors the progress of each task in relation to the contracts in place and dynamically changes the permissions of the roles where appropriate.

6 Implementation Approach

The test bed used to experiment with the concepts investigated by GOLD is built using Web Services (WS) technologies and follows the principles of service-orientation [10-14]. Each company/partner in a GOLD virtual organisation is represented as a service and communication between them is facilitated through the exchange of messages. Here we describe the design part of the GOLD test bed that deals with the task-based access control issues discussed in this paper.

6.1 Representing Tasks Using Context

Since a task may span any number of services within a particular virtual organisation, information needs to be propagated in messages so that the receiving services can determine the scope of the interaction. The context-based approach to scoping message exchanges are used in a number of WS specifications (e.g., WS-SecureConversation [15], WS-Coordination [16], WS-AtomicTransaction[17], etc.). Industry vendors have proposed WS-Context [18] as a standard way for representing context-related information, its management, and its inclusion in messages. In GOLD, we propose the use of WS-Context (or a similar specification) to model a task that spans services. A GOLD task will be represented by a context structure which would be propagated with every message being exchanged within the scope of that task. Since a GOLD service may be used by many VOs at the same time, each VO has to be identified through a context structure and since a VO may have multiple tasks, each one is represented by a context structure. There is a parent-child relationship between a VO context and a task context. Furthermore, a task may be composed of sub-tasks, so the context structure needs to support this. Listing 1 shows an example of a pseudo XML structure to represent the interaction context within GOLD.

```
<wsctx:context>
  <gold:vo>
    <!-- General information about the VO or just an
identifier or a reference. -->
    <gold:task>
      <!-- General information about the task or just an
identifier or a reference. -->
      <!-- Perhaps some sub-tasks -->
    </gold:task>
  </gold:vo>
</wsctx:context>
```

Listing 1. Pseudo XML structure of the context for message exchanges within a GOLD VO

6.2 Security

A combination of WS technologies [19] could be used to meet GOLD's security requirements. For example, WS-Security [20] defines the mechanisms for exchanging security tokens, message signing, and message encryption. WS-Trust [21] can be used when retrieving security tokens for authentication/authorisation purposes from trusted sources, WS-Federation [22] for federating identities and security attributes across different trust realms, SAML [23] for defining security assertions, XACML [24] for describing authorisation policies and making policy-based decisions, etc.

Here we are concentrating only on the task-based access control aspects of security and those specs that we can use for our implementation. We propose that XACML is used within GOLD to define access policies on objects/resources for authorisation purposes (what actions are allowed to be performed on a resource by roles) while each role can be represented using SAML assertions. Security-related information associated with a requestor (the user belonging to a role) can be propagated with every message so that services can reason about the requestor's security-related claims and determine, based on policy assertions, whether access to local resources should be granted within the scope of the particular task. We achieve task-based access control through the dynamic association of the SAML assertions with the context.

6.3 Example

An example of a pseudo SOAP [25] message carrying context and security information is presented in Listing 2.

```
<soap:Envelope>
  <soap:Header>
    <wsse:Security>
      <wsse:BinarySecurityToken>
        <!-- X.509 certificate -->
      </wsse:BinarySecurityToken>
      <saml:Assertion>
        <!-- Assertions about the requestor's roles
             (e.g., Chemist, Manager, etc.) -->
      <saml:Assertion>
    </wsse:Security>
    <wsctx:context>
      <gold:vo>
        <!-- information about the VO. -->
        <gold:task>
          <!-- information about the task. It could be just
an identifier.
             It may contain sub-tasks. -->
        </gold:task>
      </gold:vo>
    </wsctx:context>
  </soap:Header>
  <soap:Body>
    <gold:ChemicalAnalysisRequest>
      <!-- Task-specific information -->
    </gold:ChemicalAnalysisRequest>
  </soap:Body>
</soap:Envelope>
```

Listing 2. A pseudo SOAP message in GOLD carrying context and security information

When a GOLD service receives a message like the one of Listing 2, it uses the SAML assertions about the role of the requestor and the context representing the VO and the task being performed in that VO to determine whether the request can be satisfied. The decision may use a Policy Decision Point (PDP) as per the SAML specification [23].

In the example of Listing 2, we can assume that the message is signed using the X.509 certificate of the requestor and encrypted using the X.509 certificate of the receiving service, as per the WS-Security [20] specification. Also, WS-

SecureConversation [15] could be used to improve upon the performance of a multi-message conversation. Lastly, a SAML authentication-specific context could be used to replace the need for X.509 certificates and, hence, allow a federated authentication scheme to be adopted within GOLD.

7 Conclusion

In this paper we discussed task based access control as a mechanism for dynamic virtual organisation scenarios where roles and access right policies continuously evolve according to the contracts put in place. Traditional role based models are static and therefore inadequate in such modern dynamic environments. We proposed a solution based on concepts such as spheres of control and coordinated atomic actions to structure our system so that trust emerges as a system property. Current WS standards enables us to quickly develop such a mechanism as we can map our conceptual elements on standardised XML schemas and WS protocols. Furthermore they allow us to dynamically manage access rights depending on the progress of a particular activity such as a transaction. Access rights can therefore be awarded or withdrawn depending on progress.

References

1. T. Anderson, A. Avizienis, and W. Carter, "Dependability: Basic Concepts and Terminology," in Series: Dependable Computing and Fault-Tolerant Systems Volume 5, J.-C. Laprie, Ed. New York: Springer-Verlag, 1992.
2. G. Coulouris and J. Dollimore, "Security Requirements for Cooperative Work: A Model and its System Implications," presented at 6th Workshop on ACM SIGOPS European Workshop: Matching Operating Systems to Application Needs, Wadern, Germany, 1994.
3. K. T. Roshan and R. S. Sandhu, "Task-Based Authorization Controls (TBAC): A Family of Models for Active and Enterprise-Oriented Authorization Management," presented at IFIP TC11 WG11.3 Eleventh International Conference on Database Securty XI: Status and Prospects, 1997.
4. R. S. Sandhu, E. J. Coyne, H. L. Feinstein, and C. E. Youman, "Role-Based Access Control Models," *IEEE Computer*, vol. 29, pp. 38-47, 1996.
5. R. K. Thomas, "Team-based Access Control (TMAC): A Primitive for Applying Role-based Access Controls in Collaborative Environments," presented at Second ACM Workshop on Role-based Access Control, Fairfax, Virginia, United States, 1997.
6. P. Periorellis and J. E. Dobson, "Case Study Problem Analysis. The Travel Agency Problem," University of Newcastle upon Tyne, Newcastle upon Tyne, UK 2001.
7. C. T. Davies, "Spheres of Control," *IBM Systems Journal*, vol. 17, pp. 179-198, 1978.
8. A. Romanovsky, "Coordinated Atomic Actions: How to Remain ACID in the Modern World," *ACM SIGSOFT Software Engineering Notes*, vol. 26, pp. 66-68, 2001.
9. A. F. Zorzo, P. Periorellis, and A. Romanovsky, "Using Coordinated Atomic Actions for Building Complex Web Applications: a Learning Experience," presented at 8th IEEE International Workshop on Object-oriented Real-time Dependable Systems (WORDS 2003), Guadalajara, Mexico, 2003.

10. "Service-Oriented Architecture (SOA) Definition."
    http://www.service-architecture.com/web-services/articles/
    service-oriented_architecture_soa_definition.html.
11. D. F. Ferguson, T. Storey, B. Lovering, and J. Shewchuk, "Secure, Reliable, Transacted
    Web Services: Architecture and Composition."
    http://msdn.microsoft.com/webservices/default.aspx?pull=/library/en-us/dnwebsrv/html/
    wsoverview.asp, 2003.
12. H. He, "What is Service-Oriented Architecture."
    http://webservices.xml.com/pub/a/ws/2003/09/30/soa.html, 2003.
13. S. Parastatidis, J. Webber, P. Watson, and T. Rischbeck, "WS-GAF: A Grid Application
    Framework based on Web Services Specifications and Practices." Submitted for publica-
    tion, 2004.
14. D. Sprott and L. Wilkes, "Understanding Service-Oriented Architecture."
    http://msdn.microsoft.com/library/en-us/dnmaj/html/aj1soa.asp, 2004.
15. "Web Services Secure Conversation Language (WS-SecureConversation)."
    http://msdn.microsoft.com/ws/2004/04/ws-secure-conversation/, 2004.
16. "Web Services Coordination (WS-Coordination)."
    http://msdn.microsoft.com/ws/2003/09/wscoor, 2003.
17. "Web Services Atomic Transaction (WS-AtomicTransaction)."
    http://msdn.microsoft.com/ws/2003/09/wsat, 2003.
18. OASIS(WS-CAF), "Web Services Context (WS-CTX)."
    http://www.iona.com/devcenter/standards/WS-CAF/WSCTX.pdf.
19. J. Rosenberg and D. Remy, *Securing Web Services with WS-Security*. Indianapolis: Sams
    Publishing, 2004.
20. OASIS, "Web Services Security (WS-Security)."
    http://www.oasis-open.org/committees/wss.
21. "Web Services Trust Language (WS-Trust)." http://msdn.microsoft.com/ws/2004/04/ws-
    trust/, 2004.
22. "Web Services Federation Language (WS-Federation)."
    http://msdn.microsoft.com/ws/2003/07/ws-federation/, 2003.
23. OASIS, "Security Assertion Markup Language (SAML) v2.0."
    http://www.oasis-open.org/committees/security, 2004.
24. OASIS, "Extensible Access Control Markup Language (XACML)."
    http://www.oasis-open.org/committees/xacml.
25. W3C, "SOAP Version 1.2 Part 1: Messaging Framework," in *W3C Recommendations*, M.
    Gudgin, M. Hadley, J.-J. Moreau, and H. F. Nielsen, Eds., 2003.

Self-deployment of Distributed Applications

Ichiro Satoh

National Institute of Informatics
2-1-2 Hitotsubashi, Chiyoda-ku, Tokyo 101-8430, Japan
Tel: +81-3-4212-2546, Fax: +81-3-3556-1916
ichiro@nii.ac.jp

Abstract. This paper presents a framework for aggregating Java-based distributed applications from one or more mobile components that can travel between computers. The framework enables components to specify their own relocation policies and dynamically deploys them at the same or different computers according to the policies. It also provides mobile-transparent communications between components. It can dynamically organize and execute an application on a group of one or more computers to satisfy its requirements beyond the limited capabilities of individual computers. This paper also describes a prototype implementation of the framework and its applications.

1 Introduction

The complexity of modern distributed systems has already frustrated our ability to deploy components at appropriate computers through traditional approaches, such as centralized and top-down techniques. It is difficult to adapt such systems to changes in execution environments, such as adding or removing components and network topology, and to the requirements of users. This problem becomes more serious in ubiquitous computing as well as large-scale distributed systems, because ubiquitous computers are heterogeneous and their computational resources, such as processors, storage, and input and output devices, are limited so that they can only support their own initial applications. An application can execute on a group of one or more computers to satisfy its requirements beyond the limited capabilities of individual computers. Moreover, such a group must be configurable in run-time because the goals and positions of users may change dynamically.

To accomplish goals beyond the capabilities of individual computers, a ubiquitous computing application should not only be able to be processed by a single computer but also by the interaction of a group of computers, called a *federation*. Moreover, such a group must be configurable in runtime because users' requirements may change dynamically. This paper presents a framework that enables ubiquitous computers to be dynamically federated. The framework facilitates the construction of a virtual computer as a federation of partitioned applications around different computers. It also enables partitioned applications to be deployed at, and run on, heterogeneous computers that can provide the computational resources required by users and their associated context, such as locations, current tasks, and the number of people.

In the remainder of this paper, we describe our design goals (Section 2), the design of our framework, called Hydra, and a prototype implementation of the framework

N. Guelfi et al. (Eds.): FIDJI 2004, LNCS 3409, pp. 48–57, 2005.

(Section 3) and the programming model for it (Section 4). We present an application of the framework (Section 5). We then briefly review related work (Section 6), provide a summary, and discuss some future issues (Section 7)

2 Approach

The goal of this framework is to provide a general infrastructure that enables applications on a distributed system to be deployed dynamically. The framework enables us to construct an application as a federation of ubiquitous computers connected through a network to overcome the limitations of computational resources, such as input and output devices and restricted processors, in single ubiquitous computers (Figure 1).

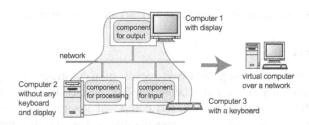

Fig. 1. Federation of heterogeneous computers

Applications and partitioned applications must not be bound to ubiquitous computers, which have limited computational resources, for various applications, but they should run on computers that can satisfy their requirements, according to changes in users and their associated contexts, e.g., locations, current tasks, and the number of people. Therefore, the framework builds partitioned applications as mobile agent-based software components and enables these to move to other computers while the application is running. When an application is made up of multiple components, the movement of one component may affect the others. It therefore provides three typical interactions: *publish/subscribe* for asynchronous event passing, remote method invocation, and stream-based communication to coordinate mobile components. It also provides mechanisms to retain these interactions even when some of the components have moved to other locations. Moreover, the deployment of components is often dependent on their applications. For example, two components are required to be at the same or nearby computers, when the first is a program that controls the keyboard and the second is one that displays content on the screen. The framework therefore enables each component to explicitly specify a policy to migrate components, called a *hook*. The policy means that a component follows another as we can see in Fig. 2. Our framework can dynamically allocate a federation of partitioned applications at suitable computers by using these policies. The current implementation provides two policies, called *attach* and *follow*.

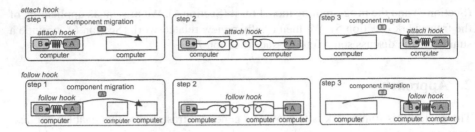

Fig. 2. Follow policy with two components

3   Design and Implementation

This framework consists of two parts: components and component hosts.

3.1   Component

It relies on the concept of component-based application construction [17], because automatically partitioning existing standalone applications across multiple computers is almost impossible. An application is loosely composed of software components, which may run on different computers. Our framework does not assume any application models unlike those in existing related work [3, 8, 18].

Each component in the current implementation is a collection of Java objects in the standard JAR file format and can migrate from computer to computer and duplicate itself by using mobile agent technology[1]. Each is also equipped with its own identifier and the identifier of the federation that it belongs to. Each also specifies the computational capability that its destination hosts must offer in composite capability/preference profiles (CC/PP) [19] form to describe the capabilities of component hosts and the requirements of components. The framework provides each component with built-in APIs to verify whether or not its destinations satisfy its requirements. The APIs transform profiles into their corresponding LISP-like expressions and then evaluate them.

3.2   Component Coordination

Each component can provide references to the other components of the application federation that it belongs to. Each reference allows a component to interact with the component that it specifies, even when the proceeding and following components are at different computers or when they move to other computers. The current implementation of referencing provides three types of mobility-transparent interactions: publish/subscribe-based remote event passing, remote method invocation, and stream communication between computers. Moreover, each reference defines two migration policies as follows:

– When a component declares an *attach* hook for another component, if the following component moves, the hook instructs the preceding one to migrate to the destination if the destination can satisfy the requirements of the component.

---

[1] JavaBeans can easily be translated into components in the framework.

– When a component declares a *follow* hook for another component, if the following
component moves, the hook instructs the preceding one to migrate to the destination
or a proper host that is near the destination that can satisfy the requirements of the
component.

The second policy is available when location sensing systems can locate computers.
Our hook mechanism seems to be similar to the dynamic layout of distributed applications in the FarGo system [5]. However, the FarGo's deployment policies aim to allow
one or more components to control another, whereas ours aim to allow one component
to describe its own migration. This is because our framework treats components as autonomous entities that travel under their own control from computer to computer. This
difference is important, because FarGo policies may conflict if two components can
declare different relocation policies for one single component, whereas our framework
is free of any conflict because each component can only declare a policy for its own
relocation instead of other components.

3.3 Component Host

Each component host is a computer, and it provides a runtime system for executing and
migrating components to other hosts. Each host establishes at most one TCP connection
with each of its neighboring hosts and exchanges control messages, components, and
inter-component communications with these through the connection.

Component Runtime Service: Each runtime system is built on the Java virtual machine,
which conceals the differences between the platform architecture of source and destination hosts, such as the operating system and hardware. Each runtime system governs
all the components inside it and maintains the life-cycle state of each component. When
the life-cycle state of a component changes, e.g., when it is created, terminates, or migrates to another host, the runtime system issues specific events to the component. This
is because the component may have to acquire various resources or release them, such
as files, windows, or sockets, that it had previously captured.

Component Migration Service: Each component host can exchange components with
another through a TCP channel using mobile agent technology. When a component is
transferred over a network, a component host on the sending side marshals the code
of the component and its state into a bit-stream and then transfers it to the destination.
Another component host on the receiving side receives and unmarshals the bit-stream.
The current implementation uses the standard JAR file format to pass components that
can support digital signatures, allowing authentication. It provides a weak migration of
components between computers by using Java's object serialization package to marshal
components. The package can save the content of instance variables in a component
program but does not support stack frames of threads being captured. Instead, when
a component is marshaled and unmarshaled, the component host propagates certain
events to its components to instruct them to stop their active threads, and then it automatically stops and marshals them after a given period of time.

Migration-Transparent Coordination Service: Remote event passing and stream-based communication in the current implementation are implemented with our original remote method invocation (RMI) mechanism through TCP connection, which is independent of Java's RMI because the original RMI lacks any reference updating mechanism in migrating components. Each component host maintains a virtually connected group of one or more components, when some components migrate to other computers. When a component migrates to another computer, it informs the current component host about the identifiers of components that may hold references to it. The component host then searches its database for the network addresses of the component hosts with the components specified in the identifiers, and it then sends *suspend* messages to these hosts to block any new uplinks from them to the migrating component. After the component arrives at the destination, it sends an *arrival* message with the network address of the destination to the departure host via the destination host. When the departure host receives the arrival message, it sends `resumption` messages with the address of the destination to component hosts with components that may hold references to the moved component to update their databases.

Relocation Policy Management Service: We will now explain to how to relocate components where those that an application consists of initially are deployed at hosts within a localized space smaller than the domain of a sub-network for multicasting packets. When a component migrates to another component host, it registers its policy with the destination host if it has the policy. The host then sends a query message to the source host of the visiting component. There are two possible scenarios for this: the visiting component has a policy for another component, and it is specified in the other components' policies. In the former scenario, because the source host knows the host running the target component specified in the policy of the visiting component, it requests this host to send destination-host information about itself and neighboring hosts that it knows, e.g., network addresses and capabilities. In the second scenario, the source host multicasts a query message within the current or neighboring sub-networks. If a host has a component whose policy specifies the visiting component, it sends the destination host information about itself and its neighboring hosts. The destination host then instructs the visiting component to migrate to one of the candidate destinations recommended by the target host.

3.4   Current Status

A prototype implementation of this framework was built with Sun's Java Developer Kit version 1.4[2]. Although the current implementation was not built for performance, we measured the group migration of three components. After a component migrates to another location, the cost of migrating another component that declares an attach policy for the moving component is 60 msec, where the cost of migrating a component between two hosts over a TCP connection is 40 msec. This experiment was done with five component hosts (Pentium III-1.2 GHz with Windows XP and JDK 1.4) connected through a Fast Ethernet network.

---

[2] Functionalities of the framework except for subscribe/publish-based remote-event-passing can be implemented on Java Developer Kit version 1.1 or later versions, including Personal Java.

4   Component Programming

Each component was implemented as a collection of Java objects. Also, each component needed to be an instance of a subclass of the `MobileComponent` class. Here, we will explain some programming interfaces that characterize the framework.

```
class MobileComponent extends MobileAgent
  implements Serializable {
  void go(URL url)
    throws NoSuchHostException { ... }
  void duplicate()
    throws IllegalAccessException { ... }
  void setComponentProfile(
    ComponentProfile cpf) { ... }
  boolean isConformableHost(
    CCPPHostProfile hp) { ... }
  ComponentProfile getComponentProfile(
    ComponentRef ref) { ... }
  setPolicy(ComponnetProfile cref,
    MigrationPolicy mpolicy) { ... }
  ComponentRef[] getGroupComponents() { ... }
  ComponentRef[] getComponents(
    Object cif) {..}
  ComponentProfile getComponentProfile(
    ComponentRef ref) { ... }
  ....
}
```

By invoking `go()` a component migrates to the destination specified as the `url` and the `duplicate()` method creates a copy of the component, including its code and instance variables. Each component can specify a requirement that its destination hosts must satisfy by invoking the `setComponentProfile()` method, with the requirement specified as `cpf`, where the requirement is defined in CC/PP form. The class has a service method named `isConformableHost()`, which the component uses to decide whether or not the capabilities of component hosts specified as an instance of the `HostProfile` class satisfy the requirements of the component.

4.1   Component Migration Programming

Each component can declare its own migration policy by invoking the `setPolicy()` of the `Component` class while it is running.

```
setPolicy(cref, new MigrationPolicy(Policy.ATTACH));
setPolicy(cref, new MigrationPolicy(Policy.FOLLOW));
```

For example, the upper command of the above code fragment means that when a component specified as `cref` moves to another computer, the component that executes the command migrates to the same computer or nearby computers in the current cell that the computer resides at. The framework is open to the introduction of new policies as long as they are subclasses of `MigrationPolicy` that define the migration policy.

4.2   Component Coordination Programming

Component references are responsible for tracking possible moving targets and for invoking the targets' methods. They are defined as the `ComponentRef` class and provide the following APIs for remote interactions. The framework provides APIs for three types of mobility-transparent interactions: publish/subscribe-based remote event passing, remote method invocation, and stream communication between computers. The first is implemented as remote method invocation for components on local or different computers with copies of arguments.

```
Message msg = new Message("print");
msg.setArg("hello world");
Object result = cref.invoke(msg);
```

This provides a generic remote publish/subscribe approach using Java's dynamic proxy mechanism, which is a new feature of the Java 2 Platform since version 1.3 [3].

```
SampleListener sl = new SampleListenerImpl();
cref.addListener(sl, "SampleListener");
```

The above code fragment registers the listener object specified as sl, which is an implementation of the SampleListener interface. The addListener() method dynamically creates a proxy object on a remote component host that has a remote component specified as cref. The proxy is an implementation of the SampleListener interface and automatically forwards events that are specified in the interface to the listener object on the local host.

The third enables two components on different hosts to establish a reliable channel through a TCP connection managed by the hosts. It is offers a subclass of Java's InputStream and OutputStream classes to mask differences between local and remote communications as much as possible. Since our channel relies on TCP, it can guarantee exactly-once communication semantics across the migration of components.

5   Experience

This section outlines a typical mobile application developed with the framework. The application is a mobile editor and is composed of three partitioned components. The first, called *application logic*, manages and stores text data and should be executed on a host equipped with a powerful processor and a lot of memory. The second, called a *viewer*, displays text data on the screen of its current host and should be deployed at hosts equipped with large screens. The third is called a *controller* and forwards texts from the keyboard of its current host to the first component. They have the following relocation policies. The application logic and control components have *follow* hook policies for the viewer component to deploy themselves at the current host of the viewer component or nearby hosts. As we can see from Figure 3, we assumed that the three components would initially be stored in the two hosts.

The system can track the movement of a user in physical space through RFID-tag technology and introduces a component, called a *user-counterpart*, that can automatically move to hosts near the current location of the user, even while the user is moving. That is, a user-counterpart is always at a host near the user. Because the viewer component has a *follow* hook policy to move the user-counterpart component, it moves to

---

[3] As the dynamic creation mechanism is beyond the scope of this paper, we have left it for a future paper.

a host that has the user-counterpart, or nearby hosts. When a user moves to another location, the components could be dynamically allocated at suitable hosts without losing any coordination between them as we can see in Figure 3.

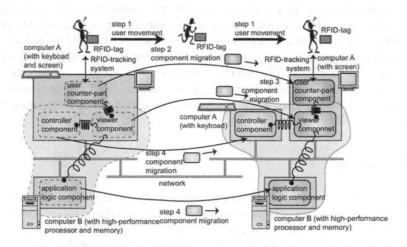

Fig. 3. Initial allocation of components for editor-application

6 Related Work

A research trend in pervasive computing is to aggregate computational resources attached to different computers. Several projects for aggregation in computers in pervasive computing settings have been explored. For example, EasyLiving [1] provides middleware for dynamically aggregating network-enabled input/output devices, such as keyboards and mice, even when they are used with to different computers. BEACH [18] is middleware for constructing collaborative applications through shared or distributed devices. Neither approach can dynamically deploy components around different computers. Aura [3] is an infrastructure for binding tasks associated with users and migrating applications from computer to computer as users move about. It focuses on providing contextual services to users rather than integrating multiple computers to support functions and performance that cannot be attained through a single computer. Gaia [8] is an infrastructure that allows applications to be partitioned between different computers and moving from computer to computer under the control of a centralized server instead of the applications themselves. Most existing approaches, including BEACH and Gaia, assume that applications are inherently designed based on the model-view-control (MVC) approach, but many modern applications are constructed based on more complex application models, e.g., design patterns, rather than the traditional MVC model. Moreover, these existing systems assume that there are centralized systems to manage computers so that they cannot support the requirement of each individual application. They are also not always scalable in widespread building-wide or city-wide systems. To solve these problems, the framework introduces the notion of relocation constraint, called the *hook* policy. This notion enables a federation of components to be organized among heterogeneous computers in a self-organized manner.

We described an infrastructure for location-aware mobile agents in a previous paper [14]. Like the framework presented in this paper, that infrastructure provided RFID-tagged entities, including people and things, with application-level software to support and annotate them. However, since it could not partition an application into one or more components, it needed to deploy and run applications on single instead of multiple computers. We presented an earlier version of the framework presented in this paper in a recent short paper [15]. The previous framework was aimed at building an application as a federation of one or more mobile components, but lacked any migration-transparent coordination mechanisms or dynamic relocation policies supported by the current framework.

7   Conclusion

This paper discussed a novel framework for dynamically aggregating distributed applications in ubiquitous computing environments. It was used to build an application from mobile agent-based components, which could explicitly have policies for their own deployment. It also supported most typical interactions between partitioned applications on different computers. It enabled a federation of components to be dynamically structured in a self-organized manner and move among heterogeneous computers that could provide the computational resources required by the components. We believe that the framework provides a general and practical infrastructure for building distributed and mobile applications. We designed and implemented a prototype system for the framework and demonstrated its effectiveness in several practical applications.

In concluding, we would like to identify further issues that need to be resolved. Security is essential in mobile applications and the current implementation of the system relies on Java's security manager. However, we plan to design a security mechanism that is more suited to distributed applications. We developed an approach to test context-aware applications on mobile computers [13], but need to develop a methodology. We are interested in developing a methodology to test distributed applications that are based on this new framework by using our new approach. We also proposed a language to specify the itinerary of mobile software [16], which enables us to define more flexible and varied policies to deploy components.

References

1. B. L. Brumitt, B. Meyers, J. Krumm, A. Kern, S. Shafer, EasyLiving: Technologies for Intelligent Environments, Proceedings of International Symposium on Handheld and Ubiquitous Computing (HUC'00), pp. 12-27, September, 2000.
2. E. Gamma, R. Helm, R. Johnson, and J. Vlissides, Design Patterns, Addison-Wesley, 1995.
3. D. Garlan, D. Siewiorek, A. Smailagic, and P. Steenkiste, Project Aura: Towards Distraction-Free Pervasive Computing, IEEE Pervasive Computing, vol. 1, pp. 22-31, 2002.
4. R. Grimm, el. al., System support for pervasive applications,
   http://www.cs.nyu.edu/rgrimm//one.world.pdf

5. O. Holder, I. Ben-Shaul, and H. Gazit, System Support for Dynamic Layout of Distributed Applications, Proceedings of International Conference on Distributed Computing Systems (ICDCS'99), pp 403-411, IEEE Computer Soceity, 1999.
6. G. E. Krasner and S. T. Pope, A Cookbook for Using the Model-View-Controller User Interface Paradigma in Smalltalk-80, Journal of Object Oriented Programming, vol.1 No.3, pp. 26-49, 1988.
7. J. A. Landay and G. Borriello, Design Patterns for Ubiqutious Computing, Computer, vol. 36, no. 8, pp. 93-95, IEEE Computer Society, August 2003.
8. M. Román, C. K. Hess, R. Cerqueira, A. Ranganat R. H. Campbell, K. Nahrstedt K, Gaia: A Middleware Infrastructure to Enable Active Spaces, IEEE Pervasive Computing, vol. 1, pp.74-82, 2002.
9. M. Román, H. Ho, R. H. Campbell, Application Mobility in Active Spaces, Proceedings of International Conference on Mobile and Ubiquitous Multimedia, 2002.
10. I. Satoh, MobileSpaces: A Framework for Building Adaptive Distributed Applications Using a Hierarchical Mobile Agent System, Proceedings of IEEE International Conference on Distributed Computing Systems (ICDCS'2000), pp.161-168, April 2000.
11. I. Satoh, Building Reusable Mobile Agents for Network Management, IEEE Transactions on Systems, Man and Cybernetics, vol.33, no. 3, part-C, pp.350-357, August 2003.
12. I. Satoh, MobileSpaces: An Extensible Mobile Agent System, IEICE Transactions on Fundamentals of Electronics, Communications and Computer Sciences, vol.E86-A, no.11, pp.2782-2790, November 2003.
13. I. Satoh, A Testing Framework for Mobile Computing Software, IEEE Transactions on Software Engineering, vol. 29, no. 12, pp.1112-1121, December 2003.
14. I. Satoh, Linking Physical Worlds to Logical Worlds with Mobile Agents, Proceedings of IEEE International Conference on Mobile Data Management (MDM'04), pp. 332-343, IEEE Computer Society, January 2004.
15. I. Satoh, Dynamic Federation of Partitioned Applications in Ubiquitous Computing Environments, Proceedings of 2nd International Conference on Pervasive Computing and Communications (PerCom'2004), pp.356-360, IEEE Computer Society, March 2004.
16. I. Satoh, Selection of Mobile Agents, Proceedings of IEEE International Conference on Distributed Computing Systems (ICDCS'2004), pp.484-493, IEEE Computer Society, March 2004.
17. C. Szyperski, D. Gruntz, and S. Murer, Component Software (2nd), Addison-Wesley, 2003.
18. P. Tandler, Software Infrastructure for Ubiquitous Computing Environments: Supporting Synchronous Collaboration with Heterogeneous Devices, Proceedings of UbiComp'2001, LNCS vol. 2201, pp. 96-115, Springer, 2001.
19. World Wide Web Consortium (W3C), Composite Capability/Preference Profiles (CC/PP), http://www.w3.org/TR /NOTE-CCPP, 1999.

Modeling and Analysis of Exception Handling by Using UML Statecharts

Gergely Pintér and István Majzik

Department of Measurement and Information Systems
Budapest University of Technology and Economics, H-1521 Budapest, Hungary
{pinterg,majzik}@mit.bme.hu

Abstract. Our paper aims at proposing a framework that allows programmers
to exploit the benefits of exception handling throughout the entire development
chain of Java programs by modeling exception handling in the abstract UML
statechart model of the application, enabling the use of automatic model checkers for checking the behavioral model for correctness even in exceptional situations, and utilizing automatic code generators for implementing the Java source
of exception-aware statecharts.

Keywords: Exception handling, UML, formal methods, model checking

1 Introduction

Using software exceptions has become the de-facto way for handling abnormal situations in software, especially since the introduction of the Java language, where exceptions are part of the language, libraries and frameworks. Despite of the popularity of
this mechanism development methods usually do not enable the developers to be
aware of exceptional situations throughout the entire development chain (modeling,
model checking and implementation).

When using the latest supported version of UML (1.5), the only way for *modeling
behavior* in exceptional situations is the implicit use of the class and interaction diagrams [1] (for modeling the exception classes and their propagation respectively). The
new major version of UML (2.0) introduces constructs for modeling exceptions in
activity and sequence diagrams. There were several *model-checking* methods introduced for validating event-driven behavioral specifications [2]. Although these methods are capable of processing most of statechart constructs, no comprehensive approach was proposed that enable the checking of behavior in exceptional situations.

Since the *implementation* of complex event-driven behavioral logic specified by
UML statecharts is labor intensive and error-prone, design patterns and code generation techniques were proposed [3, 4, 9] for automatically generating the control core
just to be customized by the programmer (i.e., implementing the necessary actions,
guard predicates etc.). Unfortunately these methods are not aware of exceptions: programmers can not use the normal exception handling mechanisms for indicating abnormal situations and initiating statechart-level handling mechanisms.

According to our knowledge, although there exist solutions for important problems
(e.g. [5, 6, 7, 10]), no general framework has been proposed that is capable of sup-

N. Guelfi et al. (Eds.): FIDJI 2004, LNCS 3409, pp. 58–67, 2005.

porting the exception handling paradigm throughout the *entire development chain* i.e., *modeling exceptions* and the handling mechanism in UML statecharts, enabling the automatic *model-checking* of the exception-aware statecharts and automatically *generating source* code where the programmer is allowed to use the standard exception throwing facilities of the language for initiating statechart-level reaction to the exceptional situation. Our paper aims at filling this gap by (1) proposing a light-weight notation for expressing the occurrence and handling of exceptions in UML statecharts, (2) discussing how to use the Extended Hierarchical Automaton notation (mathematical formalism used for model-checking statecharts) to enable the model-checking of exception-aware statecharts and (3) presenting an implementation pattern for statecharts where programmers are enabled to use exceptions for indicating exceptional situations and initiating statechart-level reaction. Although our discussion focuses on Java the implementation can be ported to other languages. The organization of our paper corresponds to the questions answered by the approach:

- *How to represent exceptions in the behavioral model and how to handle them similarly to programming language-level exception (e.g., try-catch-finally blocks, propagation etc.)?* – On one hand the *representation* of programming language-level exceptions in the statechart is achieved by catching the exceptions thrown in the programmer-written parts at the interfaces of the event dispatcher and transforming them to exception events (i.e., ordinary events in the statechart that correspond to exceptions). This approach assumes a callback-style framework organization i.e., where the programmer-written parts are called as functions by the event dispatcher. On the other hand the most important organization ideas and benefits of try-catch-finally constructs can be elevated to the *handling of exception events* by applying the statechart organization pattern suggested in this paper (Section 2).
- *How to check the exception-aware behavioral model by legacy model checkers?* – Since our approach does not modify the statechart semantics, legacy *model checkers* developed for statecharts are usable as discussed in Section 3.
- *How to implement exception-aware statecharts in Java?* – Section 4 presents an *implementation pattern* for mapping behavioral models to Java source code.

Having discussed the modeling and model checking issues and introduced the implementation pattern the final section concludes the paper and presents the directions of our future research.

2   Introducing Exceptions in the Abstract Behavioral Model

In this section we identify the *possible sources* of Java language-level *exceptions*, propose a mechanism for *transforming* them to UML *statechart events* and introduce a *pattern* (statechart design convention) for *handling the events* in the statechart similarly as exceptions are handled in Java programs.

We model event-driven systems by using UML Statecharts. The State Machine package of UML [8] specifies a set of basic concepts (states and transitions) and several advanced features (state hierarchy, orthogonal decomposition, history states etc.) to be used for modeling discrete behavior through finite state-transition systems. The operational semantics is expressed informally by the standard in terms of the operations of a hypothetical machine that implements a statechart specification.

The example discussed in this article is the traffic supervisor system in the crossing of a main road and a country road. The controller provides higher precedence to the main road, i.e., it does not wait until the normal time of switching from red to yellowred if more than two cars are waiting at the main road (the arrival of a car is indicated by a sensor). Cars running illegally in the crossing during the red signal are detected by a sensor and recorded by a camera. For simplicity reasons only the statechart diagram of the light control of the main road is investigated here (Fig. 1).

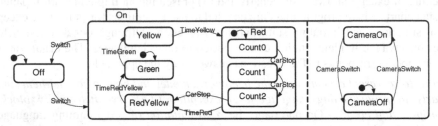

Fig. 1. Statechart of the traffic light example

2.1 Reflecting Programming Language-Level Exceptions

The throwable classes (i.e., ones that can be thrown by the *throw* Java keyword and are directly or transitively derived from the *Throwable* class) can be grouped to three main categories: (1) descendants of the *Error* class are thrown by the virtual machine (VM) on encountering a very serious problem (e.g., internal data inconsistency); (2) classes derived from the *Exception* class are used for indicating exceptional situations in the application. Java programs usually throw and catch Exceptions. Since exceptions indicate primarily exceptional situations (i.e., ones that require some handling that is different from the normal execution flow) exceptions should not be considered as fault notifications only: it is completely normal to throw and catch some exceptions (especially interface exceptions) during the execution of a Java program. The only distinguished class directly derived from the *Exception* class is the (3) *RuntimeException* class that represents non-systemic issues (i.e., ones typically resulting from application bugs like accessing objects by null reference) detected by the VM.

2.2 Transforming Java Exceptions to UML Statechart Events

Our goal is to support the modeling of exception handling using a modeling pattern based on the standard notation of statecharts. The prerequisite of this approach is to elevate exception handling to the abstraction level of statecharts by *mapping exceptions thrown in actions* (i.e. occurring in the VM or in the routines implemented by the application programmer) *to events* of the statechart. Accordingly, before presenting the modeling pattern, we will introduce this mechanism.

Taking into consideration the implementation of a UML statechart the application code can be divided into two parts: the *event handler engine* that is responsible for coordinating the behavior according to the statechart specification and the *routines implemented by the application programmer* (state entry and exit actions and actions associated to transitions, including all the libraries used by these routines). In this discussion and in the implementation pattern proposed at the end of the paper we assume a *callback-style implementation* [9] of the statechart (Fig. **2**, left): actions are methods of Java classes (called *action methods* here) and the event handler engine calls them according to the statechart specification, the configuration and the current event.

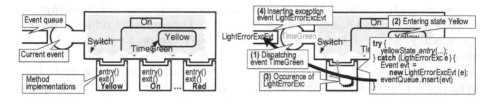

Fig. 2. Left: Callback-style statechart implementation; right: dispatching an exception thrown by an action method and transforming it into an exception event

In this point of view the *interfaces* of the action methods are the borders between the event handler engine and the programmer-written parts. Obviously the Java exceptions are to be used in the programmer-written routines as in any other applications without modifying the programming model but when reaching the event handler engine–action method interface they are to be caught since the propagation upwards the function call stack would destroy the normal operation of the event handler engine. After catching the exception an appropriate event is to be inserted in the event processing queue. All this mapping is performed in the event handler engine.

For example a safety criterion against the traffic controller can be to achieve a *fail-safe* state after the failure of one of the lights by switching off the power of all the lights in the crossing. The fault is detected by the entry actions of specific states, e.g., the entry action of the Yellow state detects a short circuit, and the appropriate code section throws a *LightErrorExc* exception. This way when the event handler engine catches an exception after calling the function implementing the entry action of state Yellow it inserts a *LightErrorExcEvt exception event* in the queue (Fig. 2, right)

This approach necessitates the discussion of two issues: (1) the transformation of exceptions to events should not interfere with the run-to-completion (RTC) semantics of the UML statechart specification and (2) the insertion of exception events in the queue should be compatible with the event queue semantics:

- The RTC semantics of UML statecharts means that an event can only be dequeued and dispatched if the processing of the previous event is fully completed. Our approach meets this requirement since (i) the insertion of a new event in the event queue does not interrupt the processing of the current event and (ii) actions can be considered to be performed even if they throw an exception since the action methods can provide a cleanup routine in a finally block if necessary.
- The UML standard does not restrict the dequeuing policy of the event dispatcher leaving open the possibility of modeling different priority schemes; in this point of view inserting an exception event in the head of the processing queue is an implementation of a priority scheme that provides high priority to exception events.

2.3 The Exception-Event Handling Pattern

The following discussion introduces a modeling pattern (statechart organization pattern) that enables the handling of exception events in a similar fashion as Java language exceptions are handled in programs. The key concepts of the exception model in Java to be implemented in UML statecharts are as follows: (1) exception handling routines are *separated* from the regular code; (2) exceptions may be *propagated* upwards the control hierarchy until an appropriate handler is found and (3) groups of exceptions can be established by organizing them in a *class refinement hierarchy*.

The exception event handling pattern introduces composite states similar to the *try-catch-finally* blocks of Java programs. The *TryBlock* composite state encloses the normal operation to be carried out without having to handle exceptional situations (Fig. 3). The *CatchBlock* composite state contains substates that enclose the activity to be performed when handling specific exceptional situations. Transitions triggered by the appropriate exception events connect the *TryBlock* composite state to corresponding substates of the *CatchBlock* composite state. The *FinallyBlock* composite state encloses the activities to be performed after the *TryBlock* regardless whether an exception event has been delivered or not; this is why transitions with empty triggers connect the *TryBlock* and *CatchBlock* composite states to *FinallyBlock*.

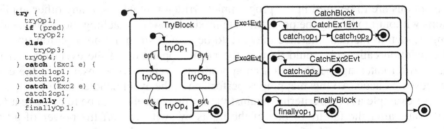

Fig. 3. The exception-event handling pattern

On the left side of Fig. 3 a Java pseudo source fragment is presented while on the right side a UML statechart that performs *similar behavior* as the Java program (note that the source is not the implementation of the statechart, just an analogy). It is easy to see that following this pattern the behavior of the statechart will be analogous to the Java exception handling semantics and provides the same key benefits:

- Since the exception handling routines are moved into composite states the *separation from the normal behavior* is even more visual than the catch blocks in Java.
- Since states can be refined to any depth, the *propagation* of Java exceptions upwards the function call stack is analogous to recursively applying the pattern (e.g., refining the state *tryOp₁* in Fig. 3 in a similar fashion). If an exception event occurs, it will trigger the transition at the deepest level of the hierarchy where a corresponding *Catch* state is defined (as the virtual machine invokes the catch block that corresponds to the function at the deepest level of the function call stack interested in handling the exception). In Fig. 4 the *Called* composite state is aware of only handling *SpecExcEvt* but since it is embedded in a structure that catches the more generic *GenExcEvt* exception event class, if a *GenExcEvt* exception event

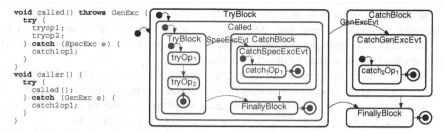

Fig. 4. Propagation of exception events

occurs in *Called*, the event triggers the transition at the higher hierarchy level and the execution continues with the appropriate catch block.

- Exception events can be organized into a class hierarchy similarly to Java exceptions. A restriction of our approach is that the order of catch blocks can not be represented in the statechart. This way one can not handle a generic exception event and an event derived from it at the same level of the statechart since according to the statechart semantics both transitions triggered by the exception events would be enabled resulting in a non-deterministic selection.

The statechart of the traffic lamp (Fig. 1) after introducing *LightErrorExcEvt exception event* as the statechart-level representation of the *LightErrorExc* exception according to the exception-event handling pattern is shown in Fig. 5.

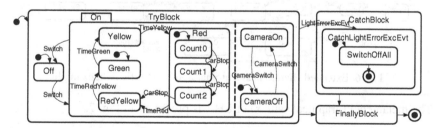

Fig. 5. Statechart of the traffic lamp after applying the exception-event handling pattern

3 Model-Checking Exception Handling

The Extended Hierarchical Automaton (EHA) notation is a well-elaborated representation of finite state-transition systems in a clear structure with formally defined semantics enabling model checking (e.g., analysis of reachability, safety and liveness properties). Since EHA are capable of representing the key modeling constructs of statecharts (state hierarchy, concurrent decomposition, interlevel transitions etc.), automatic transformations were proposed for mapping UML statecharts to EHA [11]. The *syntax* and *semantics* of EHA is described in [2]. In the following a short informal overview is given mainly focusing on the representation of UML concepts.

- An EHA consists of *sequential automata* which contain simple (non-composite) *states* and *transitions*. These states represent simple and composite states of the

UML model. States can be *refined* to any number of concurrently operating sequential automata. Composite states of the statechart can be modeled by EHA states refined to several automata representing one region each. A non-concurrent composite state is refined to only one automaton.

• Transitions may not cross hierarchy levels. Interlevel transitions of the UML model are substituted by labeled transitions in the automata representing the lowest composite state that contains all the explicit source and target states of the original transition. The labels are called *source restriction* and *target determination*. The source restriction set contains the original source states of the transition in the UML statechart while the target determination set enumerates the original target states. A transition is *enabled* if its source and all states in the source restriction set are active, the actual event satisfies the trigger and the guard is enabled. On taking the transition the target and all states in the target determination set are entered.

The EHA representation of the traffic light example after applying the exception event handling pattern (Fig. 5) is shown in Fig. 6. States of the statechart are mapped to EHA states. Concurrent and non-concurrent refinement is expressed by automata refining the appropriate states (the refinement is expressed by grey arrows in Fig. 6).

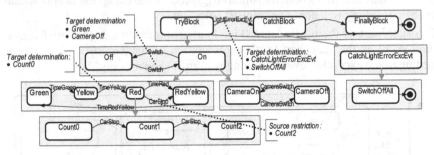

Fig. 6. Extended Hierarchical Automaton of the traffic light example

The metamodel (graphical syntax) of EHA is presented in Fig. 7.

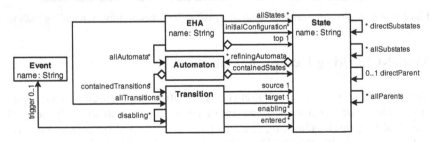

Fig. 7. Metamodel of Extended Hierarchical Automata

The EHA representation, as an abstract syntax of UML statecharts, is a basis of automatic model transformation to model checker tools [2]. Since our approach for introducing exceptions into statecharts does not modify either the statechart syntax or the semantics, only two issues are to be solved for enabling the model checking of exception-aware statecharts by the EHA-based legacy model checkers.

The first problem is to decide how to represent the hierarchy of exception events in EHA models. One solution could be to add the generalizability feature to the EHA Event concept by introducing a self-association of the Event metaclass in the meta-model, but this modification would require the corresponding modification of the EHA semantics and re-implementation of the EHA-based model checkers. In order to support legacy model checkers our approach is simply the following: if an event class E is refined to event classes R_1, R_2, ...,R_N, substitute all transitions triggered by E with a set of transitions triggered by the non-abstract event classes from the $\{E, R_1, R_2, ...,R_N\}$ set. This way the only modification needed is to implement syntactic substitutions in the tools implementing the UML statechart–EHA transformation.

The second problem is, that from the point of view of checking the behavior in exceptional situations the UML statechart model is open, since the sources of the events representing RuntimeExceptions (thrown by the Java virtual machine) and checked exceptions (thrown by routines written by the programmer) are missing. Accordingly, the model is to be closed by the verifier attaching a model of the run-time environment that generates exception events. (This step is required for model checking only.) In case of exhaustive analysis (i.e., when all possible interleaving of exceptions with normal events is considered) the generation of the model extension is a systematic process of inserting concurrent regions (where exception events are generated) to TryBlocks (where the exceptions are to be caught). The automatic implementation of this extension is a task of our current work.

4 Automatic Generation of the High-Level Behavior

This section presents our code generation pattern (Fig. 8) proposed for automatic implementation of behavioral models specified by EHA. Our goal was not only to present an approach that is capable of mapping the EHA behavior to the Java language but we were concerned in reducing the impact of the code generation pattern on the programming model followed by the developer. The pattern does not require the implementation of any interfaces or deriving active application classes from any specific base classes. This is achieved by detaching the implementation of the EHA-based behavior from the active application classes in the following way.

The *dynamic behavior* is enclosed within stateless classes that are implementations of specific EHA (i.e., they contain the corresponding structure information and all the

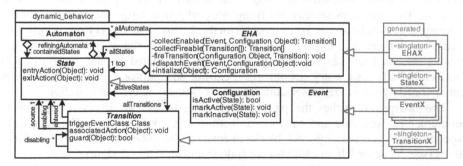

Fig. 8. Classes of the implementation pattern

callback functions implementing the actions etc.). The actual application class (e.g., the *TrafficLamp* class in case of the example) is considered as the *context* of the behavior, i.e., the application class is provided as a function parameter for the behavioral classes for accessing application-specific variables etc. This approach also necessitates active application classes to explicitly store the state configuration information since the classes implementing the behavior are stateless.

The pattern of implementing the event handler engine is essentially an interpreter consisting of two parts: the base support classes are in the *dynamic_behavior* package while the classes to be automatically generated are in the *generated* package.

From a *structural* point of view (how to represent EHA in Java) the classes *EHA*, *Automaton*, *State*, *Transition* and *Event* are the Java equivalents of the metaclasses of the EHA metamodel i.e., their instances and the associations between them are the mapping of the metamodel to the Java language.

From the point of view of the *application dynamics* (how to insert Java code into actions guards etc.), the methods of these classes are the points where the abstract concepts (actions, guards etc.) are to be filled with concrete programming language-level implementation: state entry and exit actions are methods of the *State* class (*State.entryAction, State.exitAction*) while the action associated to the transition and the guard predicate are methods of the *Transition* class (*Transition.associatedAction, Transition.guard*). Since actions and guards are specific to the concrete state and transition, these classes are abstract: their methods are to be implemented in the derived (generated) classes. The current state configuration is represented by the *Configuration* class that maintains associations to the currently active states. All active states exposing EHA-based behavior should contain an instance of this class.

The interpreter is implemented by the *EHA* class. The entry points are the *dispatchEvent* and *initialize* methods. As discussed above the active application classes acting as the context of the operation are provided as generic (*Object*) parameters to the methods. The *initialize* method is used for initializing the configuration of the active object (i.e., taking the initial transition in the UML statechart terminology). The real event dispatcher is implemented by the *dispatchEvent* function. This function is called by the application class passing the event, the configuration and the reference to itself (i.e., to the application class acting as the context of the behavior) as function arguments. The *dispatchEvent* function first calls the *collectEnabled* function that traverses the association to the *Transition* instances (role *allTransitions*) and collects the enabled transitions, then removes from this set the transitions that are disabled by priority relations (*Transition.disabling* association) by calling the *collectFireable* method. The transitions selected for firing are performed during the execution of the corresponding calls to the *fireTransition* method; this involves (1) performing the state exit actions (i.e., calling the *State.exit* methods of states enumerated by the *source* association), (2) performing the action associated to the transition, (3) performing the state entry actions (i.e., calling the *State.entry* actions of states enumerated by the *entered* association), finally (4) updating the configuration.

The interpreter catches the possibly occurring exceptions in the programmer-implemented functions and transforms them to exception events. The language-specific constructs (i.e., try-catch blocks in Java) are used here to enclose these functions (see the upper left box with source code fragment in Fig. 2 right).

The interpreter functions do not need any modification with respect to the actual behavioral model. The really critical and error-prone parts (setting up the object structure expressing the EHA) are automatically created by the code generator.

5 Summary and Future Work

Our paper has proposed a framework that supports the entire development chain of programs that exploit the benefits of exception handling. The modeling of exceptional situations is introduced to statecharts by converting the possibly occurring exceptions to events and reacting to these events in a similar fashion like Java exceptions (i.e., try-catch-finally constructs) by organizing the statechart according to our proposed pattern. Since our approach does not require the modification of the statechart semantics, legacy model checkers can be used for checking the behavior of the system even in presence of exceptions. Finally we presented our implementation pattern for source code-level instantiation of exception-aware statecharts as applied in our prototype code generators. In the near future we would like to apply our exception handling scheme for reacting to behavioral errors detected by our previously published fault detection techniques based on statechart monitoring and run-time checking of temporal logic specification.

References

1. Y. Ahronovitz, M. Huchard. Exceptions in Object Modeling. Finding Exceptions from the Elements of the Static Object Model. In A. Romanovsky et. al (eds): Exception Handling. LNCS 2022, Springer, pp 77-93, 2001.
2. D. Latella, I. Majzik, M. Massink. Automatic Verification of a Behavioural Subset of UML Statechart Diagrams Using the SPIN Model-checker. In Formal Aspects of Computing, 11(6), pp 637-664, Springer, 1999.
3. M. Samek. Practical Statecharts in C/C++. CMP Books, Kansas, USA, 2002.
4. M. Samek, P. Y. Montgomery. State Oriented Programming. Embedded Systems Programming, 2000.
5. J. D. Choi,, D. Grove. M. Hind, V. Sarkar: Efficient and Precise Modeling of Exceptions for the Analysis of Java Programs. In Proc. Program Analysis for Software Tools and Eng., 1999.
6. S. Sinha, M. J. Harrold. Analysis and Testing of Programs with Exception-Handling Constructs. IEEE Trans. on Software Engineering, 26(9), 2000.
7. G. Brat, K. Havelund, S.J. Park, W. Visser. Java PathFinder: Second Generation of a Java Model Checker. In Proc. of CAV Workshop on Advances in Verification, 2000.
8. G. Booch, J. Rumbaugh, I. Jacobson. The Unified Modeling Language User Guide. Addison-Wesley, 1999.
9. G. Pintér, I. Majzik. Automatic Code Generation based on Formally Analyzed UML Statechart Models. In Proc. Workshop on Formal Methods for Railway Operation and Control Systems, pp. 45-52, l'Harmattan, Budapest, 2003.
10. C. M. F. Rubira, R. de Lemos, G. R. M. Ferreira, F. C. Filho. Exception Handling in the Development of Dependable Component-based Systems. Software Practice and Experience. 2003.
11. D. Varró, G. Varró, A. Pataricza. Checking General Safety Criteria on UML Statecharts. In Lecture Notes in Computer Science, number 2187. Springer Verlag, 46-55. 2003.

Coordinated Anonymous Peer-to-Peer Connections with MoCha

Juan Guillen-Scholten and Farhad Arbab

Centrum voor Wiskunde en Informatica (CWI), Amsterdam, The Netherlands
{juan,farhad}@cwi.nl

Abstract. MoCha is an exogenous coordination middleware for distributed communication based on mobile channels. Channels allow anonymous, and point-to-point communication among nodes, while mobility ensures that the structure of their connections can change over time in arbitrary ways. MoCha is implemented in the *Java* language using the *Remote Method Invocation package* (RMI) [15]. In this paper we promote the use of mobile channels for P2P applications and show the benefits of the MoCha middleware.

1 Introduction

Today, a big percentage of the Internet traffic is generated by file-sharing applications. Most applications of this kind are based on a so called peer-to-peer (P2P) network. P2P networking refers to a class of systems, applications and architectures that employ distributed resources to perform any kind of task in a decentralized and self organizing way[11]. The popularity of P2P networks originates from the introduction of the Napster[5] application in the year 2000 and it is continued by many other P2P file-sharing applications like Kazaa[12], BitTorrent[4], and many clients of the Gnutella network[9].

P2P networks are often put in contrast with *client/server networks*. That is because in many network architectures each process on the network is either a client or a server: servers are processes dedicated to specific tasks like managing of disk drives, printers, or network traffic, whereas clients are processes that rely on servers for resources. The clients themselves do not share any resources. In a *peer-to-peer* architecture each node is both a client and a server at the same time. Therefore, the nodes are said to be *equal*. They have equivalent responsibilities, enabling applications that focus on collaboration and communication in a decentralized and self organizing way. Features of a peer-to-peer architecture include a better distributed network control, high availability through the existence of multiple peers in a group, and the possibility of dynamic exchange of information about the network topology.

The flexibility of P2P network architectures is increased by infrastructures that (1) allow making connections between distributed nodes across several heterogeneous platforms and operating systems, that (2) enable nodes to establish anonymous connections between them, that (3) provide some kind of mechanism

N. Guelfi et al. (Eds.): FIDJI 2004, LNCS 3409, pp. 68–77, 2005.

for easy dynamic reconfiguration of the network topology, that (4) provide exogenous coordination by letting the creator of the connection choose between a synchronous or an asynchronous type, and that (5) offer a clear and easy high-level API for P2P applications.

Such an infrastructure is the MoCha middleware[6]. In this paper we show and discuss the advantages of using MoCha for P2P applications. In the next section we give a short description of MoCha and its general concepts. Next, in section 3, we present an example of the two major types of P2P networks and how to implement them with MoCha. Finally, in section 4, we end with conclusions and related work.

2   MoCha

MoCha is an exogenous coordination middleware for distributed communication and collaboration using mobile channels as its medium. In this section we first introduce the general notion of a mobile channel and discuss its major features. Then, we give a set of mobile channel types supported by MoCha. Finally, we present MoCha's application programming interface (API).

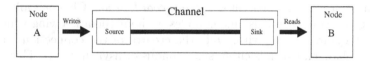

Fig. 1. General View of a Channel

2.1   Mobile Channels and Their Features

A channel, see figure 1, consists of two distinct ends: usually (*source, sink*) for most common channel-types, but also (*source, source*) and (*sink, sink*) for special types. These channel-ends are available to the processes that constitute a *node*. Processes can *write* by inserting values to the source-end, and *read* by removing values from the sink-end of a channel; the data-flow is locally *one way*: from a process into a channel or from a channel into a process.

Channels are *point-to-point*, they provide a directed virtual path between the nodes involved in the connection. Therefore, using channels to express the communication carried out within a system is *architecturally very expressive*, because it is easy to see which nodes (potentially) exchange data with each other. This makes it easier to apply tools for analysis of the dependencies and data-flow.

Channels provide *anonymous connections*. This enables P2P client applications to exchange messages with other applications without having to know *where* in the network those other applications reside, *who* produces and consumes the exchanged messages, and *when* a particular message was produced or will be consumed. Since the applications do not know each other, it is easy to update or exchange any one of the nodes without the knowledge of the node at the other side of the channel.

The ends of a channel are *mobile*. We introduce here two definitions of mobility: logical and physical. The first is defined as the property of passing on channel-end identities through channels themselves to other nodes in the system; spreading the knowledge of channel-ends references by means of channels. The second is defined as physically moving a channel-end from one location to another location in a distributed system, where location is a *logical address space* where node processes execute. Both kinds of mobility are supported by MoCha.

Because the communication via channels is also *anonymous*, when a channel-end moves, the node at the other side of the channel is not aware nor affected by this movement. Mobility allows dynamic reconfiguration of channel connections among the component nodes in a system, a property that is very useful and even crucial in systems where the components themselves are mobile. A component is called mobile when, in a distributed system, it can move from one location (where its code is executing) to another. Laptops, mobile phones, and mobile Internet agents are examples of mobile components. The structure of a system with mobile components changes dynamically during its lifetime. Mobile channels give the crucial advantage of moving a channel-end together with its component, instead of deleting a channel and creating a new one.

Channels provide transparent *exogenous coordination*. Channels allow several different types of connections among nodes without them knowing which channel types they are dealing with. Only the creator of the connection knows the type of the channel, which is either synchronous or asynchronous. This makes it possible to coordinate nodes from the 'outside' (exogenous), and, thus, change the systems behavior without changing the nodes.

2.2   Channel Types Supported by MoCha

MoCha supports eleven types of channels. Here we give a short description of five representative channel types. For more details and the remaining channel types we refer to the MoCha manual [6].

- *Synchronous channel.* The I/O operations of the two ends are synchronized. A *write* on the source-end can succeed only when simultaneously a *take* operation is performed on the sink-end, and vice-versa. A *take* operation is the destructive version of the *read* operation.
- *Lossy synchronous channel.* If there is no I/O operation performed on the Sink channel-end while writing a value to the Source-end, the *write* operation always succeeds but the value gets lost. In all other cases, the channel behaves like a normal synchronous type.
- *Filter (synchronous) channel.* The Filter channel behaves like a *synchronous* type. However, values that do not match the channel's pattern are filtered out (lost). *Write* operations where the value is filtered out of the channel have no influence on, nor are they influenced by, *take* operations that are performed on the same channel.

- *Asynchronous unbounded FIFO channel.* The I/O operations performed on both channel-ends are done in an asynchronous way. Values written into the Source channel-end are stored in the channel in a FIFO distributed buffer until taken from the Sink-end.
- *Asynchronous bounded FIFO (FIFO n) channel.* This channel behaves in the same way as the unbounded FIFO one, except that is has a capacity of n elements. If the channel is full a *write* operation has to wait until an element is taken out of the channel first.

2.3   MoCha's Implementation and API

MoCha is implemented in the *Java* language using the *Remote Method Invocation package* (RMI) [15] and comes in three different flavors: *MoCha, easyMoCha* and *chocoMoCha.*

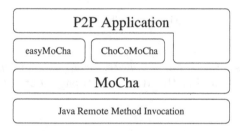

Fig. 2. The MoCha Middleware

As indicated in figure 2, *MoCha* is the basic package build upon the *RMI* layer. *MoCha* contains all the features needed to properly work with channels. However, non-experts find it difficult to work with this basic package due to two reasons. One is that the user interface is rather short and meant for expert programmers. The other reason is that in this basic MoCha package dangling references may occur due to channel-end movement. This means that the user has to write its own protocol for dealing with these invalid channel-end references. This is our intention since the choice for a particular protocol depends on the kind of system one wants to build. For non-experts or people who simply do not want to be concerned with such things we have developed *easyMoCha.* This layer is build on top of MoCha and has all the features of plain MoCha plus: a more richer and easier to use interface, and a build-in protocol for taking care of invalid channel-end references. We have also developed a package that has more or less the same features as *easyMoCha* but with the addition that nodes have to first successfully connect to a channel-end before being able to use it. We call this package *chocoMoCha* (channel connection MoCha).

The middleware has a clear and easy high-level application programming interface (API). In figure 3 we list the main classes of *MoCha* with their most

method	parameters	return	description
MoChaLocation: MoCha needs a location that points to a particular IP and Virtual Machine.			
constructor	()	void	creates a location.
equals	(MoChaLocation loc)	boolean	compares the given location with this one.
SourceEnd: The source-end of a channel.			
write	(Object element)	void	writes data or a channel-end reference.
SinkEnd: The sink-end of a channel.			
read	(void)	Object	reads an element and leaves it in the channel.
take	(void)	Object	destructive version of read.
ChannelEnd: An abstract class implemented by Source- and Sink-end.			
move	(MoChaLocation loc)	void	moves channel-end to loc.
equals	(ChannelEnd ce)	boolean	compares the ce with this one.
equalsChannel	(ChannelEnd ce)	boolean	does ce belong to the same channel?
empty	(void)	boolean	is the channel empty?
full	(void)	boolean	is the channel full?
MobileChannel: An instance holds two ChannelEnd references.			
constructor	(MoChaLocation loc, String type)	void	creates a new channel.

Fig. 3. MoCha API

important operations: *create channel*, *write*, *read*, *take*, and *move*. Full API details can be found in [6] and at the MoCha web page (`http://homepages.cwi.nl/~juan/MoCha/`).

3   P2P Applications on Top of MoCha

In this section we show the advantages of using MoCha for P2P applications. We discuss the two current architecture types for P2P networks. These are the *hybrid* and the *pure* P2P network architectures as defined in [11]. We explain how to implement both P2P architectures using mobile channels by giving an example of each them.

In a *hybrid* P2P network there is always a *central entity* necessary that provides parts of the offered network services. Such a central entity is often regarded as a server in the traditional way. However, the definition of a hybrid P2P architecture is not equal to the one of the client/server architecture; All the nodes of the first potentially share resources, while the clients of the second do not.

Figure 4 shows a *hybrid* P2P network that uses mobile channels for connections between its nodes. This network example is similar to the one of the Napster application[5]. Each *application node* has a set of resources to share among the other nodes of the network. However, an application node does not know any other nodes, nor the resources these other nodes are sharing. Instead, an application node connects to a *central index server* that contains a list of all the resources available from all the nodes connected to it. Once a node receives a list of resources from the *server* and requests a particular resource, the *server* arranges a connection between the requesting- and the providing-node.

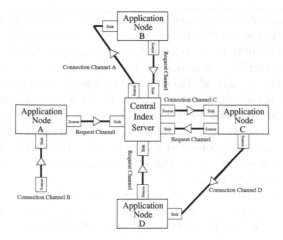

Fig. 4. A Hybrid P2P Network

```
class P2PApplicationNode
   P2PApplicationNode (SourceEnd ce)
      requestSource = ce;
      location = new MoChaLocation();
      connection = new MobileChannel(location,"Synchronous");
   connect()
      // connection.ce1 = source-end
      // sharelist = list of resources we share.
      if (!connection.ce1.full()) {
         Message msg = new Message("Joining network", connection.ce1, shareList);
         requestSource.write(msg); }
      else { // find another server or try later. }
   getResource(String resource)
      // connection.ce2 = sink-end
      Message msg = new Message("Request", resource, connection.ce1);
      requestSource.write(msg);
      while(!finished) {
         msg = connection.ce2.take();
         result.add(msg); } //done
class centralizedIndexServer
   centralizedIndexServer()
      location = new MoChaLocation();
      request = new MobileChannel(location, "FIFO 100");
   void performConnect()
      msg = request.ce2.take(); // request.ce2 = sink-end
      shareList.add(msg.shareList, msg.source);
      msg.source.move(location); // move conn. chan. source-end to us.
      msg.source.write(new Message("Connected to server"));
   void performGetResource()
      msg = request.ce2.read(); // request.ce2 = sink-end
      Node tmp = shareList.getRandomNodeWith(Resource);
      msg.source.move(node.location); // move conn. chan. source-end to resource node.
      tmp.source.write(msg); // msg already contains target SourceEnd.
```

Fig. 5. Partial Abstract Java Code of a Hybrid P2P Network

Implementing this example in MoCha is fairly easy. In figure 5 we show the most important methods of a possible implementation. Figure 4 shows a snapshot of our example network. The server has several *request channels*. The sink-ends of these channels are kept private by the server and are meant for reading requests. However, the source-end references are known to all the application nodes in order for them to write requests to these channels. Since, in our example, the server is always on-line the nodes get a source-end reference at their creation, see their `constructor` method. Each application node has a *connection channel* meant for receiving data from the outside world, it does so by reading from the sink-end of this channel. The nodes spread the reference of the source-end to the server when connecting to it, as specified in the method `connect`. Suppose that node A is in the process of connecting to the server, then node B represents the resulting state. The server moved the source-end to its location and wrote an acknowledgment message back.

At some point in time node B requests a resource, see the `getResource` method. The server, in response, reads the request but it does not take it out of the channel, see the `performGetResource` method. Instead, the server looks randomly for a node that has the requested resource and moves the *connection source channel-end* to the found application node. This is the state represented by the nodes D and C. Node C receives a resource request from the server that was written by node D. The request remained in the channel unaffected by the channel-end move and without node D begin aware of it. Since the request also contains the target source-end, node C writes the data to it. However, it does not know that node D is receiving the data, nor does node D know that it is getting the requested data from node C. Therefore, the connection is *completely anonymous*.

To illustrate the advantage of exogenous coordination: we chose the types of the *request channels* and the *connection channels* to be respectively *asynchronous FIFO* and *synchronous*. However, we could choose other channel types as well, if desired. For example, we can make the *request channels* to be of type *synchronous*. This way, we get a different system behavior with the big advantage of not having to change, nor re-compile, the code of the application nodes. Moreover, the nodes don't even know with what kind of channel type they are dealing with.

A *pure* P2P network has no *central entity*, it is completely decentralized. Figure 6 shows a *pure* P2P network that uses mobile channels for connections between its nodes. This network example is similar, but not entirely the same, to the Kazaa network[12]. Actually, the implementation of this example is also similar to the one of the *hybrid* network example. That is why, due to space limitations, we do not present any code for this example. Most of the functionality is already given in figure 5.

Instead of having a fixed central server, we now have *supernodes*. A *supernode* is a normal application node, but at the same time it performs some of the tasks of the *server* in the *hybrid* example; it keeps a resource-list of the connected clients, and it arranges connections between the different connected nodes in the same manner as the server did. For legal reasons, the nodes cannot share any resources of the supernode they are connected too, and vice-versa.

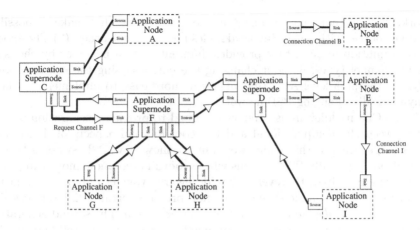

Fig. 6. A Pure P2P Network

A supernode itself is a normal node connected to another supernode. Any node can become a supernode and back to normal depending on the network state and heuristics. This means that nodes need a dynamic list of supernode source-ends, for if the supernode they are connected to becomes unavailable. To keep its list updated a node can request source-end references of neighbor nodes from its supernode. However, to keep network traffic down, a node can connect to only one supernode at the same time.

In figure 6 nodes E and I are connected to supernode D, nodes C, D, G and H are connected to supernode F, node A is connected to supernode C, and node B is not connected to any supernode. In this snap-shot nodes E and I are the only ones involved in resource transfer; node E is writing data to the connection channel of node I. The anonymous connection between the two nodes is made by supernode D in the same way as the index server in the hybrid network example.

In this *pure* P2P network the topology changes more than the one in the previous example. This more dynamically changing network example clearly shows the benefits of the mobility feature of MoCha's channels. Instead of creating and deleting channels every time a topological change occurs, we just simply move its ends to other nodes. When moving one end, the nodes using the other end of the channel are not even aware of the channel-end movement.

Just like in the previous example, we can change the network's behavior by choosing different types for the channels between the nodes. All of this is done in an exogenous way.

4 Related Work and Conclusion

In this paper we introduced and promoted the use of the MoCha middleware for P2P networks. The examples in section 3 showed the advantages of using MoCha for both a *centralized* and a *decentralized* P2P network. The advantages include, (1) the mobility of channel-ends to cope with dynamic changes in the network. (2) The anonymous connections between nodes, that makes it possible to share resources without the involved nodes knowing each other. (3) The exogenous coordination feature, that provides different system behavior by choosing different channel types, without changing the entities using the channel. And, finally, (4) the high-level API, that makes it more easy to implement, update, and dynamically changing P2P networks.

The MoCha middleware is primary designed to provide a separation of concerns between the computational and the coordination aspects of distributed systems in general. In this paper we want to show how P2P systems benefit from MoCha. Especially P2P systems where coordinated anonymous exogenous connections are desired. However, our middleware provides only a coordination mechanism (mobile channels) and does not provide certain P2P services like *searching for particular data, load balance,* and *indexing.* The second generation of P2P middleware offers a complete package for such systems. Well-known middlewares are *Chord* [13], *Pastry* [10], *Tapestry* [16], and *CAN* [8]. They all provide means for locating nodes and data in the network, as well as efficient and scalable routing protocols of messages. However, they do not provide explicit (exogenous) coordination between the nodes. Therefore, designers using these middlewares can still profit from MoCha by making prototypes of their systems using mobile channels to explicitly show the coordination aspects of these systems. Later they can implement MoCha's mobile channels in these second generation P2P middlewares (if desired).

Shared data spaces are another kind of coordination mechanism. With this mechanism nodes read and write values, usually tuples like in *Linda* [3], from and to a shared space. The tuples contain data, together with some conditions. Any nodes satisfying these conditions can read a tuple; tuples are not explicitly targeted. In [2] an infrastructure for P2P networks is suggested using the Linda middleware Lime [7]. However, we think that for most P2P networks it is more efficient to use MoCha's point-to-point channels than the centralized shared data spaces.

MoCha relates to the JXTA project [14]. The JXTA middleware provides a set of protocols that have been designed for *ad hoc,* pervasive, and multi-hop peer-to-peer network computing. The JXTA protocol most closely related to MoCha is the *Pipe Binding Protocol.* In contrast to MoCha channels, pipes provide the illusion of a virtual in and out mailbox that is independent of any single peer location, and network topology (multi-hops route).

MoCha strongly relates to Reo[1], an exogenous coordination language where complex channel connections are compositionally build out of simpler ones. Reo provides high-level connection specifications whose semantics are independent of the entities using the connection.

References

1. F. Arbab, *A channel-Based Coordination Model for Component Composition,* Tech. Report, Centrum voor Wiskunde en Informatica, Amsterdam, 2002. Available online at http://www.cwi.nl/

2. N. Busi, C. Manfredini, A. Montresor, G. Zavattaro, *Towards a Data-driven Coordination Infrastructure for Peer-to-Peer Systems*, Proc. of Workshop on Peer-to-Peer Computing Co-located with NETWORKING'02, 2002.
3. N. Carriero, D. Gelernter. *How to Write Parallel Programs: a First Course*, MIT press, 1990.
4. B. Cohen, *Incentives Build Robustness in BitTorrent*, Technical Report, May 22, 2003. Available at `http://bitconjurer.org/BitTorrent/documentation.html`
5. drscholl@users.sourceforge.net, *Napster Messages*, on-line document, April 7, 2000. Available on-line at `http://opennap.sourceforge.net/napster.txt`
6. J.V. Guillen-Scholten, F. Arbab, *MoCha and easyMoCha Manual v1.0*, CWI Technical Report, Amsterdam, 2004.
7. A.L. Murphy, G.P. Picco, and G.-C. Romjan. *Lime: A coordination middleware supporting mobility of hosts and agents.* Technical Report WUCSE-03-21, Washington University, Department of Computer Science, St. Louis, MO (USA), 2003.
8. S. Ratnasamy, P. Francis, M. Handley, R. Karp, S. Shenker, *A Scalable Content-Addressable Network*, ACM SIGCOMM '01, San Diego, 2001.
9. M. Ripeanu,*Peer-to-Peer Architecture Case Study: Gnutella Network*, Technical Report, University of Chicago, 2001. S. Ratnasamy, P. Francis, M. Handley, R. Karp, S. Shenker: A Scalable Content-Addressable Network; ACM SIGCOMM '01, San Diego, 2001.
10. A. Rowstron, P. Druschel, *Pastry: Scalable, Decentralized Object Location and Routing for LargeScale Peer-to-Peer Systems*, 18 Conference on Distributed Systems Platforms, Heidelberg (D), 2001.
11. R. Schollmeier, *A Definition of Peer-to-Peer Networking towards a Delimitation Against Classical Client-Server Concepts*, Proceedings of EUNICE-WATM, pp. 131-138, Paris, France, September 3-5, 2001.
12. Sharman Networks, *Kazaa, Detailed On-line Guide*, On-line Manual, 2003. Available at `http://www.kazaa.com/us/help/guide.htm`
13. I. Stoica, R. Morris, D. Karger, M. F. Kaashoek, and H. Balakrishnan, *Chord: A Scalable Peer-to-peer Lookup Service for Internet Applications*, ACM SIGCOMM 2001, San Diego, CA, August 2001, pp. 149-160.
14. Sun Microsystem Inc., Home Page of the JXTA project, `http://www.jxta.org`
15. Sun Microsystems Inc., *Java Remote Method Invocation – Distributed Computing for Java*, white paper available at `java.sun.com/rmi`, 2004.
16. B. Y. Zhao, J. D. Kubiatowicz, and A. D. Joseph. Tapestry: An infrastructure for fault-resilient wide-area location and routing. Technical Report UCB//CSD-01-1141, U. C. Berkeley, April 2001.

A Survey of Software Development Approaches
Addressing Dependability

Sadaf Mustafiz and Jörg Kienzle

School of Computer Science, McGill University, Montreal, Quebec, Canada
sadaf@cs.mcgill.ca, joerg.kienzle@mcgill.ca

Abstract. Current mainstream software engineering methods rarely consider dependability issues in the requirements engineering and analysis stage. If at all, they only address it much later in the development cycle. Concurrent, distributed, or heterogeneous applications, however, are often deployed in increasingly complex environments. Such systems, to be dependable and to provide highly available services, have to be able to cope with abnormal situations or failures of underlying components. This paper presents an overview of the software development approaches that address dependability requirements and other non-functional requirements like timeliness, adaptability and quality of service. Software development methods, frameworks, middleware, and other proposed approaches that integrate the concern of fault tolerance into the early software development stages have been studied. The paper concludes with a comparison of the various approaches based on several criteria.

1 Introduction

Due to the increasing responsibilities and number of requirements that modern applications have to address, the average complexity of software systems is growing. Elaborate user interfaces, multi-media features or interaction with real-time devices require software to respond promptly and reliably. Situations such as node failures, network partitions, overloaded resources, irregular load, component failures, heterogeneity, abnormal behavior of subsystems or the environment, and also software design faults must be handled in order to provide highly available services.

Surprisingly enough, dependability and fault tolerance are not addressed by current mainstream software engineering methods. In general, dependability and fault tolerance are considered "non-functional" requirements, and therefore considered too late during the development of an application. Ad-hoc solutions that try increase dependability by adding fault tolerance once the main functionality of the system has been implemented often result in complex system structure, hard-to-maintain code and poor performance.

This paper summarizes the results of a survey of specialized software development methods, frameworks, middleware, software architectures, and other approaches that assist developers in producing dependable software. Dependability can be attained by fault prevention, fault removal, fault tolerance[1] and fault forecasting [3]. The investi-

---

[1] An overview of software fault tolerance techniques can be found in [36].

N. Guelfi et al. (Eds.): FIDJI 2004, LNCS 3409, pp. 78–90, 2005.

gation focuses on the non-functional requirements that are part of dependability, i.e. availability, reliability, safety, security, and maintainability [2], but also timeliness, which includes responsiveness, orderliness, freshness, temporal predictability and temporal controllability [29]. Adaptability, i.e. the need to remain functional even when modifications are carried out in the system, is also considered. In addition the review includes, for each approach, its application environment, the covered failure domain, and what fault tolerance techniques, if any, have been incorporated into the process.

The approaches presented in this paper are structured into three categories. Section 2 reviews *software development methods*. Section 3 discusses *software architectures, middlewares* and *frameworks*. Section 4 presents other approaches that propose notations or consider elements that help in the development of dependable systems. Finally, Section 5 presents a comparison of the surveyed approaches.

2 Software Development Methods

Software development methods define a step-by-step process that leads a developer from the elaboration of an initial requirements document, over analysis, architecture and design phases through to the final implementation.

2.1 HRT-HOOD

HOOD (Hierarchical Object-Oriented Design) [32] is an architectural design method developed by the European Space Agency in 1987, with Ada as the target programming language. HRT-HOOD (Hard Real-Time HOOD) [9] was later developed to addresses issues of timeliness in the early stages of the development process, with explicit support for common hard real-time abstractions. HRT-HOOD introduces cyclic and sporadic type objects to take into account timing properties of real-time systems. These objects are annotated with information about the period of execution, minimum arrival time, offset times, deadlines, budget times, worst-case execution time (WCET), and importance. HRT-HOOD uses exceptions to handle timing faults. The coding language should have support available to program recovery handling. In cases of sporadic objects, method invocation should be monitored in order to prevent early execution or overly high invocation frequency. The method does not provide fault-tolerance support or ways of identifying the mentioned non-functional requirements, but focuses on how to integrate them into the design phase. The STOOD tool supports real-time software development based on the HOOD (version 4) and HRT-HOOD method.

2.2 The OOHARTS Approach

Object-Oriented Hard Real Time System (OOHARTS) [35] is a process for developing dependable hard real-time systems. It is based on UML and the hard real-time constructs of HRT-HOOD. Various extensions to UML are proposed, e.g. stereotypes such as <<cyclic>>, <<aperiodic>>, <<protected>>, <<passive>>, and <<environ-

ment>> to describe different real-time objects. A special form of UML state diagram called Object Behavior Chart (OBC) is used to define object behavior. It provides means for representing timing constraints like deadline and period. The UML concurrency attribute, which can be sequential, guarded, or concurrent, is extended to include <<mutex>> (mutual exclusion), <<wer>> (write execution request), and <<rer>> (read execution request).

The OOHARTS method follows the traditional software development phases. Both functional and non-functional requirements are specified in the requirements definition phase. It introduces an additional phase in the HRT-HOOD software development life cycle, hard-real time analysis, which provides a framework for defining the structure and behavior of hard real-time systems using UML and the new extensions defined [35].

2.3   Extension of the Catalysis Method

In [31], a fault-tolerant software architecture for component-based systems based on the *idealized fault-tolerant component (IFTC)* [38][44] is proposed. The architecture can handle software faults, providing higher levels of dependability.

Based on this work, [45] proposes a way of incorporating exception handling and error recovery into the Catalysis [17] process. At the requirements level, exceptional behavior, which includes recovery scenario and failure scenario, is added to use-case specifications in a formal manner. The system is structured with IFTC and the propagation of exceptions is clearly modeled. In the next phase, collaborations are derived from the use-cases. Pre- and post conditions are mapped to actions, which include refinements of the defined exceptions. A template is used to describe the collaboration, and class hierarchies of normal and exceptional behavior are produced. Following the design, ways to move on to implementation are suggested.

2.4   The KAOS Approach

The KAOS framework [22] provides a goal-oriented approach for requirements modeling, specification, and analysis, which address both functional and non-functional requirements. Three types of non-functional goals are considered: quality-of-service, development, and architectural constraints. These goals address the need for safety, security, usability, performance, interoperability, accuracy, maintainability, reusability, and issues of distribution, and physical and logical organization. Exceptional behavior, defined as *obstacles*, is also addressed during requirements engineering [48]. Goals and obstacles are expressed in a formal language. Based on this framework, Lamsweerde has proposed a method in [49] for deriving the software architecture from the requirements. To begin with, the software specification is developed from the requirements, which is then used to build the architectural design. The design evolves with recursive refinements, which consider constraints and non-functional goals. The refinement is pattern-based; Figure 1 for example shows how to introduce reliable communication by means of replication. The KAOS approach is supported by the GRAIL tool [22].

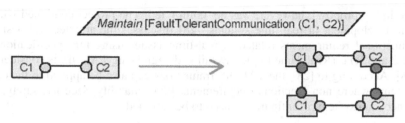

Fig. 1. Architectural refinement pattern for a QoS goal [49]

2.5 The B Method

The B formal method [1] covers the development process from the specification to the implementation phase and is based on a mathematical model of set theory and first order logic. The B method mainly comprises two activities: writing formal texts and proving the texts. The process evolves from specification to coding using a series of refinements. The methodology has been used for developing error-free software for critical systems by focusing on traceability of safety-related constraints [10]. The method is supported by the tools B-Toolkit and Atelier-B. Modeling tools (B4free), editors, and parsers are also available for B.

3 Fault Tolerance Frameworks and Middleware

This section reviews software architectures, middlewares and frameworks. *Software architectures* do not offer any methodological support, but instead provide a structure (usually hardware design) based on which applications can be built. *Middleware* is software that is used to integrate heterogeneous software applications or products efficiently and reliably in a distributed computing environment. It is the middle layer between the application program and the platform and provides abstractions necessary for interfacing. A *framework* is an environment composed of software components that can be tailored according to the needs of the application being developed. Finally, a *middleware framework* is a structure that offers users multiple middleware styles that can be customized for application as well as device constraints.

3.1 TARDIS

The **Timely and Reliable Distributed Information Systems (TARDIS)** project [8] was initiated in 1990, and is targeted towards avionics, process control, military, and safety critical applications. The proposed framework addresses non-functional requirements (dependability, timeliness, and adaptability), and implementation constraints from the early stages of software development. In the architectural design phase, issues of choices are addressed, for example, between replication and dynamic reconfiguration for improving reliability. The framework is generic, and does not impose any software design methods or languages on the developer.

The initial proposal, however, was not completed. The project continued with focus on development of real-time systems. [28] discusses the architectural design of non-functional requirements related to real-time issues using the specification language Z and RTL (Real-Time Logic). Detailed design using TARDIS is considered in [7][28]. According to [28], the TARDIS framework can also be applied to the design of systems where non-functional requirements like reliability, security, safety, fault tolerance, and system reconfiguration need to be satisfied.

3.2 TIRAN

TaIlorable fault toleRANce frameworks for embedded applications (TIRAN) [20] is a European Strategic Program for Research in Information Technology (ESPRIT) project completed in October 2000. The primary goal of the project was to develop a software framework to provide fault tolerant capabilities to embedded automation systems. The framework, to reduce development costs, aims to solve problems in fault-affected applications by considering error detection, isolation and recovery, reconfiguration and graceful degradation. It considers physical and design faults in the permanent, temporary omission and byzantine failure domains.

The framework provides a library of basic tools implementing fault tolerance mechanisms like watchdog, distributed memory, local voter, output delay, stable memory, distributed synchronization and time-out management. A control backbone, which functions as a middleware, extracts information about the application's topology, its progress and its status. It maintains this information in a replicated database and coordinates fault tolerance actions at runtime via user-defined recovery strategies. A domain-specific language named ARIEL was developed as part of the project to configure the basic tools and to specify the recovery strategies. More information about ARIEL can be found in [20].

TIRAN provides the users of the framework with a methodology for collecting, specifying, and validating fault tolerance requirements, with a characterization of framework elements, and guidelines for using the framework. The specification of fault tolerance is based primarily on UML package diagrams and class diagrams, and TRIO (Tempo Reale ImplicitO) temporal logic, a language that has been developed by ENEL (Italy's largest power distributer) specifically for real-time systems. The use of the methodology has been experimented on a pilot application, a primary substation automation system, and is discussed in [18][25].

3.3 DepAuDE

Dependability for embedded **Au**tomation systems in **D**ynamic **E**nvironments with intra-site and inter-site distribution aspects (DepAuDE) [24] is an IST (Information Society Technologies) project partially based on TIRAN completed in 2003. It has been developed primarily for two target application areas: monitoring/control of energy transport and distribution, and distributed embedded systems.

The DepAuDE framework provides "a methodology and an architecture to ensure dependability for non-safety critical, distributed, embedded automation systems with both IP (inter-site) and dedicated (intra-site) connections" [21]. The methodology support is similar to that outlined in TIRAN, but includes inter-site communication features for specification, validation, and modeling of requirements. It also adds support for quality-of-service (QoS) levels. Furthermore, the DepAuDE framework has been applied on the pilot applications to evaluate and show the feasibility of the framework.

3.4 EFTOS: FT Approach to Embedded Supercomputing

Embedded Fault-Tolerant Supercomputing (EFTOS) is an ESPRIT project completed in 1998, targeted towards industrial process-control, real-time applications, and embedded systems. It aims to provide a middleware framework to implement fault-tolerance to make embedded supercomputing applications more dependable.

Similar to TIRAN, EFTOS also follows a layered approach comprising of basic fault-tolerance tools and mechanisms, a backbone, and a high-level recovery language for specifying recovery strategies [23]. The FT tools provided include a watchdog timer, a trap handler for exception handling, an atomic action tool, assertions, and a distributed voting mechanism.

3.5 Middleware Architectures

DCE (Distributed Computing Environment), **DCOM** (Distributed Component Object Model), **Java RMI** (Remote Method Invocation), and **CORBA** (Common Object Request Broker Architecture) are general middleware that have limited fault tolerance support, like mechanisms for replication and time-outs [46]. TAO (The ACE ORB) implementation of CORBA supports fixed-priority real-time scheduling. Electra, another CORBA implementation, provides fault-tolerance with object replication. Real-time CORBA 1.0 supports QoS with standard policies and techniques [46]. CORBA also defines a transaction service (OTS).

Chameleon is an adaptive infrastructure, which supports multiple fault-tolerance strategies in a networked environment. Chameleon uses reliable agents that support user-specified levels of fault-tolerance. It considers satisfying dependability in terms of availability. With some additional features, chameleon can be used for real-time applications [19][4].

ROAFTS is a middleware architecture providing real-time object-oriented adaptive fault-tolerance support. ROAFTS offers fault-tolerance schemes that can be applied to both process-structured and object-structured distributed real-time (RT) applications. These schemes are used to tolerate processor faults, communication link faults, interconnection network faults, and application software faults. ROAFTS is meant for implementation on COTS (Commercial Off-The-Shelf) and guarantees RT fault-tolerance when required [19][37].

FRIENDS (Flexible and Reusable Implementation Environment for your Next Dependable System) is a software architecture, which provides fault-tolerance and limited security support. It is built on subsystems and libraries of meta-objects. There is a fault-tolerance sub-system that incorporates fault-tolerance mechanisms for error detection, failure detectors, replication, reconfiguration, and stable storage. It does not provide specific support for real-time and quality-of-service requirements [19][27].

AQuA (Adaptive Quality of Service for Availability) is an adaptive architecture for building dependable distributed systems. Fault tolerance is provided by Proteus, a dependability manager integrated into the architecture. Fault tolerance support is given to CORBA applications with replication of objects, and different levels of desired dependability and quality-of-service are provided. AQuA is capable of handling crash failures, value faults, and time faults. It incorporates means for detecting errors, treating faults, and reliable communication [19][14].

3.6 Software Architectures

Some architectures considering fault-tolerance and other dependability attributes worth mentioning are discussed below. Because of space constraints, it was not possible to describe them in details.

Delta-4 [5], an ESPRIT project, provides an open architecture for development of dependable distributed real-time systems. Delta-4 tolerates hardware failures with hardware and software redundancy, and also supports active and passive replication of software components residing in homogeneous computers. Voting mechanisms and systematic and periodic strategies for check-pointing are provided.

MAFTIA (Malicious and Accidental Fault Tolerance for Internet Applications) is a European Union project completed in 2003 and is said to be the first project to address the need to tolerate malicious and accidental faults in large-scale distributed systems [39].

GUARDS (Generic Upgradeable Architectures for Real-Time Dependable Systems) [41] is an ESPRIT project aiming to provide methods, techniques, and tools for design, implementation, and validation support in safety-critical real-time systems.

MARS (Maintainable Real-Time System) [43] is an architecture specialized for time-triggered applications, and addresses fault-tolerance with active replication means and other hardware FT measures to satisfy hard real-time requirements.

3.7 Other Frameworks

This section presents some software frameworks that were came about to aid in development of dependable systems.

HIDE (High-level Integrated Design Environment for Dependability), an ESPRIT project, addressed the need for early validation of UML-based design [6]. In [12], Chin proposes an approach, as part of HIDE, to extend UML towards a useful OO-Language for modeling dependability features. It provides abstractions to incorporate common dependability requirements in the UML model.

Aurora Management Workbench provides a software framework for developing reliable, scalable, and configurable distributed applications [10].

DOORS is a framework developed to provide support for building fault-tolerant applications in CORBA [30].

4 Other Related Work

This section reviews work that addresses the need to integrate dependability requirements in the model specifications.

4.1   Developing Safety Critical Systems with UML

It is crucial when developing safety-critical systems to consider means to achieve the highest level of dependability. In [33], a technique is presented which is based on using the UML extension mechanisms to incorporate safety requirements in a UML model. The mechanisms consider crash/performance failures and value failures which may cause message loss, delay, or corruption. For example, the stereotype <<risk>> can be used to describe a risk that arises in the physical level with the tag {failure} and <<error handling>> provides an object for handling errors in the subsystem level and is associated with the tag {error object}. The approach also considers analyzing the UML model with a prototypical XMI-based tool to check if it satisfies the requirements [33]. The approach considers non-functional requirements during the design phase in terms of safety. Jürgens has also proposed using UML to develop security-critical systems in [34]. Previously, he has also, in collaboration with others, described some approaches for systems development using UML, which consider various criticality requirements.

4.2   A Framework for Integrating Non-functional Requirements into Conceptual Models

In [15], an interesting approach is presented addressing the need to capture non-functional requirements (NFR) at the early stages of development, by integrating NFR into conceptual models, specifically into the entity-relationship (ER) and object-oriented (OO) models. The proposed method describes the use of the LEL (Language Extended Lexicon) [15], and a NFR taxonomy to elicit the requirements. A comprehensive taxonomy of NFR can be found in [13]. A LEL-NFR tool is required that captures terminologies relevant to the target field, referred to as the UoD (Universe of Discourse). This tool along with the NFR taxonomy is used to derive the NFR knowledge-base for a particular domain. These NFR are decomposed and represented in graphs which a slight variants of Chung's NFR graphs [13]. Finally, the NFR are integrated into the conceptual models. In ER models, a NFR is shown in a rectangle with the UoD labeled over it, and connected to the relevant entity or relationship. In the OO model, NFR are added to class diagram by attaching two rectangles to the right bottom of the class with the UoD name in one and the NFR name in the other.

In [16], this approach has been applied to UML, starting from use cases to class diagrams, sequence diagrams, and collaboration diagrams.

5   Survey Results

This section shows a comparison of the major approaches discussed in this paper based on some important non-functional requirements. The requirements considered have been introduced in Section 1: *dependability*, *timeliness*, *adaptability*, and *quality-of-service (QoS)*. Dependability refers to availability, reliability, safety, confidentiality, integrity, and maintainability [2]. Availability and reliability can be together classified as "avoidance or minimization of service outages" [2]. Also, a specialization of availability and integrity with respect to authorization, and confidentiality can be grouped together as the *security* requirement [2]. The approaches have been evaluated based on the requirements that are satisfied or taken into consideration, and a comparison is illustrated in Table 1.

Table 1. Comparison Based on NFR

	Availability/ Reliability	Safety	Security	Maintainability	Timeliness	Adaptability	QOS	Comments
HOOD	✗	✗	✗	✓	✓	✗	✗	limited maintainability (only exception handling); timeliness (only SRT);
HRT-HOOD	✓	✓	✗	✓	✓	✓	✗	limited maintainability (only exception handling and maybe replication); adaptability (mode changes);
TIRAN	✓	✓	✗	✓	✓	✓	✗	assumes reliable communication; safety (only by criticality level)
DepAuDE	✓	✓	✓	✓	✓	✓	✓	considers intra- and inter-site communication; safety (only by criticality level)
TARDIS	✓	✓	✓	✓	✓	✓	✗	not targeted to specific NFR – open framework
OOHARTS	✓	✓	✗	✓	✓	✓	✗	limited maintainability (exceptions); adaptability (mode changes);
EFTOS	✓	✗	✓	✓	✓	✓	✗	security (integrity); timeliness (esp. SRT);
DELTA-4	✓	✗	✓	✓	✓	✗	✗	user-specified level of dependability; maintainability (only replication);
Chameleon	✓	✗	✗	✓	✗	✓	✗	supports different levels of availability requirements; adaptability (mode changes);
ROAFTS	✓	✓	✗	✓	✓	✓	✗	guarantees RT FT; adaptability (mode changes); survivability;
FRIENDS	✓	✓	✓	✓	✗	✗	✗	security (communication);
AQuA	✓	✗	✗	✓	✗	✓	✓	user-specified level of availability;

Table 2 presents a comparison of the fault-tolerance support in each approach and is classified based on the failure domain, error processing, and fault treatment support. The main techniques considered in each approach have also been mentioned.

6 Conclusion

This paper presented an assortment of methods, frameworks, middleware, architectures, and other development techniques that address dependability, timeliness, adaptability, or other QoS requirements. Due to space reasons, none of the addressed approaches have been discussed in much detail. The interested reader is encouraged to consult the detailed review given in [40].

The software development methods, HRT-HOOD and OOHARTS, consider real-time issues in isolation. The KAOS and B formal methods address dependability issues, and present a high-level approach for specifying requirements and deriving the

Table 2. Fault Tolerance Support

	Failure Domain		Error Processing	Fault Treatment	Means
	Value	Timing			
HOOD	✗	✗	detection	no support	exception processing, deadlock avoidance techniques
HRT-HOOD	✗	✓	detection	reconfiguration	exception processing, replication
TIRAN	✓	✓	detection, localization, recovery	diagnosis, masking confinement, dynamic reconfiguration, graceful degradation	exception handling, design diversity, stable memory, watchdog, local voter, distributed synchronization, time-out, standby sparing, recovery blocks, NMR
	computing failures only				
DepAuDE	✓	✓	same as above	same as above	same as above & group communication
TARDIS	✓	✓	detection, recovery	diagnosis, isolation, confinement, reconfiguration	timeout, HW/SW repair/replacement, NMR, failure messages
OOHARTS	✗	✓	detection	reconfiguration	exceptions, timeout, deadlock avoidance techniques
EFTOS	✓	✓	detection, isolation, recovery	masking, fault-tolerance	exception handling, watchdog, atomic actions, distributed voting, recovery language
DELTA-4	✓	✓	detection, recovery	reconfiguration, fault-tolerance	active/passive/leader-follower replication, voting, timeout
Chameleon	✓	✓	detection, recovery	masking, system reconfiguration, failure recovery	reliable agents, TMR (H/W), checkpoints, voting (distributed & majority)
ROAFTS	✓	✓	detection, recovery	fault-tolerance	watchdog timer, predictable communication, process scheduling, backward recovery (SRT), forward recovery (HRT), recovery blocks; active replication
FRIENDS	physical crash failures only		detection, recovery	reconfiguration, fault-tolerance	leader-follower-replication, stable storage, primary backup, failure suspectors, group communication
AQuA	✓	✓	detection, recovery	fault-tolerance, system reconfiguration	active/passive replication & degree, voting, monitors, group communication

design based on refinements. The frameworks TIRAN and DepAuDE are two significant contributions to the development of dependable systems, but cater to a specific domain. The TARDIS project provides a general framework that addresses various non-functional requirements, but does not define a step-by-step development process. Similarly, middleware infrastructures like EFTOS and ROAFTS provide FT tools that the users can adapt according to their needs. Software architectures, like DELTA-4, Chameleon, FRIENDS, and AQuA, attempt to provide hardware fault tolerance by supporting techniques like replication, but they do not provide guidelines to the user for making design decisions during software development. Several other approaches propose extension mechanisms to integrate non-functional requirements into design models, and stereotypes have been defined that add dependability-related notions to UML. However, these approaches concentrate on one particular phase, and do not provide the necessary continuity throughout the development life cycle. In short, the survey shows that there is a lot more work to be done to make dependability, and in particular fault tolerance, an integral part of software development.

References

1. Abriel, J.-R.: *The B-book*, Cambridge University Press, 1996.
2. Avizienis, A., Laprie, J.-C., et al.: "Dependability of computer systems: Fundamental concepts, terminology, and examples", in *Proc. 3rd IEEE Information Survivability Workshop (ISW-2000)*, Boston, Massachusetts, USA, October 24-26, 2000, pp. 7-12.
3. Avizienis, A., Laprie, J.-C., Randell, B.: "Fundamental Concepts of Dependability", CS-TR: 739, Department of Computing Science, University of Newcastle, 2001.
4. Bagchi, S, Whisnant, K., et al.: "Error Detection and Recovery in Chameleon", Center for Reliable and High-Performance Computing, Coordinated Science Laboratory, University of Illinois at Urbana-Champaign, Nov 98, presentation .
5. Barrett, P.A.: "Delta-4: An open architecture for dependable systems", in *IEE Colloquium on Safety Critical Distributed Systems*, 1993, pp. 2/1-2/7.
6. Bondavalli, A., Cin, M.D., et al.: "Dependability Analysis in the Early Phases of UML Based System Design", *International Journal of Computer Systems - Science & Engineering*, Vol. 16 No. 5, Sep 2001, pp. 265-275.
7. Burns, A., Lister, A. M., McDermid: "TARDIS: an architectural framework for timely and reliable distributed information systems", in *Proc. Sixth Australian Software Engineering Conf.*, Sydney, Australia, July 1991, pp. 1-15.
8. Burns, A., Lister, A. M.: "A framework for building dependable systems", *The Computer Journal*, Vol. 34 No. 2, April 1991, pp. 73- 181.
9. Burns, A., Wellings, A.: *HRT-HOOD: a structured design method for hard real-time Ada systems*, Elsevier Science BV, 1995, ISBN 0-444-82164-3.
10. Buskens. R, Siddiqui A., et al.: "Aurora Management Workbench", Bell laboratories, 2003, http://www.bell-labs.com/project/aurora.
11. Carnot, M., DaSilva, C., et al.: "Error-free software development for critical systems using the B-Methodology", in *Proc. of 3rd International Symposium on Software Reliability Engineering*, Oct 1992, pp. 274-281.
12. Chin, M.D.: "Extending UML towards a useful OO-language for modeling dependability features", in *the Ninth IEEE Workshop on Object-Oriented Dependable Real-Time Systems*, October 2003.
13. Chung, L., Nixon, B.A., et al.: *Non-functional Requirements in Software Engineering*, Kluwer Academic Publishers, 2000.
14. Cukier, M., Ren, J., et al.: "AQuA: An Adaptive Architecture that Provides Dependable Distributed Objects", in *Proceedings of the 17th IEEE Symposium on Reliable Distributed Systems (SRDS.98)*, Indiana, SA, October 20-23, 1998, pp. 245-253.

15. Cysneiros, L.M., Leite, J.C.S.P, et al.: "A Framework for Integrating Non-Functional Requirements into Conceptual Models", *Requirements Engineering Journal*, Vol. 6, Issue 2, Apr. 2001, pp. 97-115.
16. Cysneiros, L.M., Leite, J.C.S.P: "Non-Functional Requirements: From Elicitation to Conceptual Model", *IEEE Transactions on Software Engineering*, May 2004.
17. D'Souza, D., Wills, A. C.: *Objects, components, and frameworks with UML: The Catalysis Approach*, Addison-Wesley: Reading, MA, USA, 1998.
18. D1.1 - Requirement specification V2, TIRAN Project Deliverable, October 1999, confidential.
19. D2.1 and D2.2: Updated Investigation, evaluation, and selection, DepAuDE Deliverable, 2002.
20. D7.9 – Project Final Report, TIRAN Project Deliverable, October 2000, confidential.
21. D8.6: Final Report, DepAuDE Deliverable, 2003.
22. Darimont, R., Delor, E., et al.: "GRAIL/KAOS: An Environment for Goal-Driven Requirements Engineering", in *Proc of. ICSE'98 - 20th Intl. Conf .on Software Engineering*, Kyoto, Vol. 2, April 1998, pp. 58-62.
23. Deconinck, G., De Florio, V., et al.: "The EFTOS approach to dependability in embedded supercomputing", *IEEE Transactions on Reliability*, Vol. 51, Mar. 2002, pp. 76–90.
24. DepAuDE project website, April 22, 2004, http://www.depaude.org/
25. Dondossola, G., Botti, O.: "System fault tolerance specification: proposal of a method combining semi-formal and formal approaches", in *Proc. of Int. Conf. FASE2000, part of ETAPS2000 - The European Joint Conferences on Theory and Practice of Software*, Berlin, D, March 2000, LNCS, No. 1783, Springer-Verlag, Berlin, Heidelberg, New York, 2000, pp. 82-96.
26. European Dependability Initiative: Inventory of EC Funded Projects in the area of Dependability, Issue 2.2, 11 January 2000.
27. Fabre, J.-C., Pérennou, T.: "A Metaobject Architecture for Fault Tolerant Distributed Systems: The FRIENDS Approach", *IEEE Trans. on Computers*, Jan. 1998, pp. 78-95.
28. Fidge, C.J., Lister, A.M.: "A disciplined approach to real-time systems design", *Information and Software Technology*, Vol. 34 No. 9, September 1992, pp. 603-610.
29. Fidge, C.J., Lister, A.M.: "The challenges of non-functional computing requirements", in *Seventh Australian Software Engineering Conference (ASWEC'93)*, Sydney, September 1993, pp. 77-84.
30. Gokhale, A., Natarajan, B., et al.: "DOORS: Towards high-performance fault-tolerant CORBA", in *Proc. 2nd Intl. Symp. Distributed Objects and Applications (DOA '00)*, Sept. 2000.
31. Guerra, P. A. de C., Rubira, C., et al.: "Fault-Tolerant Software Architecture for Component-Based Systems", in R. de Lemos, C. Gacek, A. Romanovsky (Eds). Architecting Dependable Systems, *LNCS* 2677, Springer, 2003, pp. 129-149.
32. HOOD Reference Manual, Issue 4, 1995. Available at ftp://ftp.estec.esa.nl/pub/wm/wme/HOOD/HRM4.tar.gz.
33. Jürgens J.: "Developing safety-critical systems with UML", in *Proc. UML 2003 Conference, LNCS* 2863, Springer-Verlag 2003, pp. 360-372, San Francisco, California, USA.
34. Jürgens, J.: *Secure Systems Development with UML*, Springer-Verlag, 2004 (to be published).
35. Kabous, L., Nebel, W.: "Modeling Hard Real Time Systems with UML The OOHARTS Approach", in *Proc. UML'99 Conference, LNCS* 1723, pp. 339-355, Springer-Verlag, 1999.
36. Kienzle, J.: "Software Fault Tolerance: An Overview", in *Ada-Europe '2003, LNCS* 2655, Springer-Verlag, 2003, pp. 45-67.

37. Kim, K.H.: "ROAFTS: A Middleware Architecture for Real-time Object-oriented Adaptive Fault Tolerance Support", in *Proc. of IEEE CS 1998 HASE Symp.*, Washington, D.C., Nov. 1998, pp. 50-57.
38. Lee, P.A., Anderson, T.: "Fault Tolerance - Principles and Practice", *Dependable Computing and Fault-Tolerant Systems*, Springer Verlag, 2nd ed., 1990.
39. MAFTIA project website, http://www.newcastle.research.ec.org/maftia/.
40. Mustafiz, S.: "Addressing Fault Tolerance in Software Development: A Comparative Study", M.Sc. Thesis, School of Computer Science, McGill University, June 2004.
41. Powell, D., Arlat, J., et al.: "GUARDS: A generic upgradable architecture for real-time dependable systems", in *IEEE Trans. Parallel and Distributed Syst.*, Vol. 10, June 1999, pp. 580–597.
42. Pullum, L.L.: *Software Fault Tolerance Techniques and Implementation*, Artech House, Inc., Boston, 2001.
43. Randell, B., Laprie, J.-C., et al. : ESPRIT Basic Research Series: Predictably Dependable Computing Systems, Springer-Verlag, 1995.
44. Randell, B., Xu, J.: *The Evolution of the Recovery Block Concept*, Chapter 1, pp. 1 – 21, in Lyu, M. R. (Ed.): *Software Fault Tolerance*, John Wiley & Sons, 1995.
45. Rubira, C.M.F., de Lemos, R., et al.: "Exception handling in the development of dependable component-based systems", in *Software – Practice and Experience*, 2004. To appear.
46. Tirtea, R., Deconinck, G.: "A Survey of Middleware and its Support for Fault Tolerance", in *Proc. 6th Int. Conf. Engineering of Modern Electric Systems (EMES-2001)*, Felix-Spa, Romania, May 24-26, 2001, 6 pages.
47. UML Revision Task Force. OMG UML Specification v. 1.5. OMG Document ad/03-03-01. Available at http://www.uml.org, 2003.
48. van Lamsweerde, A.: "Building Formal Requirements Models for Reliable Software", in *Proc. of 6th International Conference on Reliable Software Technologies, Ada-Europe 2001, LNCS* 2043, Springer-Verlag, 2001.
49. van Lamsweerde, A.: "From System Goals to Software Architecture", in *Formal Methods for Software Architectures*, M. Bernardo & P. Inverardi (eds), LNCS 2804, Springer-Verlag, 2003, pp. 25-43.
50. Verentziotis, E., Varvarigou, T., et al.: "Fault tolerant supercomputing: a software approach", *International Journal of Computer Research*, Vol. 10, No. 3, Nova Scotia Publishers Inc., 2001, pp. 401-413.

FreeSoDA: A Web Services-Based Tool to Support Documentation in Distributed Projects

Frank Padberg

Fakultät für Informatik, Universität Karlsruhe
Am Fasanengarten 5, 76131 Karlsruhe, Germany
padberg@ira.uka.de

Abstract. FreeSoDA is a distributed document management system written in C# under .NET. FreeSoDA offers Web services for storing and extracting any kind of document (such as source files, plain text files, PDF files, UML diagrams, or JPEG files) to and from a central database over the Internet. Users can link related documents with each other in the database. To allow distributed simultaneous changes to the document database, FreeSoDA implements sessions with authentication and encryption on top of the stateless SOAP protocol. In addition, FreeSoDA implements an event-notification scheme which makes changes to the database immediately visible to other users.

1 Introduction

In many software projects, the documentation quickly falls behind development. One can often hear complaints by developers that documentation is useless because it is severely outdated. Instead of relying on written specification and design documents, developers often must study the code to find out how the software is structured and how it works. Some improvement has been achieved with UML tools such as TogetherJ where code and diagrams are two sides of a coin, but that covers only a fraction of the documents in a project. In addition, linking together documents which are related to each other is not supported.

The problem of how to organize the exchange of documentation is even more pressing in *distributed* projects where communication is often hampered by different time zones, cultural, geographic, and organizational barriers, and by a breakdown of informal communication channels [1]. For example, the developer community in open source projects typically is limited to communicating via mailing lists and newsgroups. Web sites such as SourceForge allow access to the CVS repository for the code base and are augmented by FAQ lists, manuals, and bug tracking systems such as Bugzilla.

To better support developers with their documentation task in distributed projects, we have developed FreeSoDA, a Web services-based document management system. FreeSoDA comes with server code and a rich client. The server manages a set of documents of arbitrary type, including source code files, Word documents, plain text files, PDF files, UML diagrams, JPEG files, and so on.

N. Guelfi et al. (Eds.): FIDJI 2004, LNCS 3409, pp. 91–100, 2005.

The client uses the Web services offered by the FreeSoDA server to allow a user to retrieve, add, and delete documents in the database.

Documents can be linked together in the database by the user in order to express some sort of relationship between the documents. For example, the files which contain the source code for several classes of the application being developed could be linked to another document which contains a UML diagram describing the interaction of these classes. Or, several design and code documents could be linked to a text document containing the specification. FIGURE 1 shows part of a client window displaying some documents in a FreeSoDA database and the links between them.

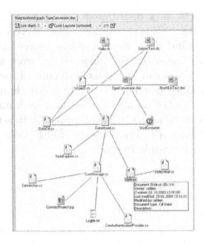

Fig. 1. Some documents linked in a FreeSoDA database

The server can handle multiple clients simultaneously. To make the communication between the server and clients efficient, we have implemented a *session scheme* on top of the (otherwise stateless) Web services. This scheme resembles the well-known observer design pattern. When the database contents change, the clients get *notified* and then fetch only a delta to their cache, which limits the amount of data which is transmitted in the system. By using a notification scheme, documents inserted or changed by one user are readily visible to other users. The same holds if the link structure in the database changes, for example, by inserting a new link between two documents. If a user is currently offline, the client will get notified about the change the next time a session is opened.

Documents carry attributes such as owner and creation date, and the same is true for the links between the documents. The server offers different *views* onto the database. A view shows only part of the full set of documents and links. The idea is to make it easier to digest and manage large collections of related documents by suitably restricting what is shown on the screen. For example, a view might show only the source files and documentation for one particular release of the code. To define a view, the project administrator specifies "filter rules" for the document and link attributes. Users can only select views which have been defined by the project administrator and for which they have been granted access.

The server can handle several projects at the same time, each having its own set of linked documents, user group, and views. We have developed an access control scheme based on user accounts and user groups to protect projects against each other. Users must authenticate themselves to the server in order to open a session and get access to the data. Guest accounts are possible. To make the communication between the server and client safe, the contents of all messages are encrypted. Instead of using one of the proposed encryption facilities for SOAP, we have developed a special encryption scheme based on the SHA256 algorithm [2] in order to avoid storing or transmitting user passwords in readable form at any time, including the time when the user account is created.

The server stores the meta-data for the documents (their attributes and location) and the link information in a SQL database. The documents themselves usually are stored in folders on the server, but may also be stored remotely; in that case, the server holds Web links to the remote documents. All information about the different projects, user groups, and access rights is also stored in the SQL database.

Our current implementations of the FreeSoDA server and client are written in C# under .NET. The server software runs on Windows 2003 Server and the Microsoft IIS. The databases run on Microsoft SQL Server. The client software runs on Windows 2000 or XP. Due to the generic design of the software, ports to Java and other Web and SQL servers should be possible.

2   Topology

The FreeSoDA system logically consists of a central FreeSoDA server, one or more project servers, one or more SQL databases, and client workstations. FIGURE 2 shows the topology of a typical, distributed setup for a FreeSoDA system.

The FreeSoDA server stores central information about the users and projects in the system. The server machine must run the FreeSoDA server code inside a Web server, such as Microsoft IIS, and offer a central URL for entry into the system. All data is persistently stored in a SQL database such as Microsoft SQL Server. The SQL database may run on the same machine as the FreeSoDA server, but in order to gain performance the database usually runs on a separate machine.

A project server stores information about the documents and links in this project, that is, meta-data and the project graph structure. In addition, a project server stores the definitions of the views which are available in the project and implements the access control for each view. Similar to the central FreeSoDA server, each project server machine must run the FreeSoDA server code inside a Web server. Each project server has a companion SQL database which may run on the same machine, but usually runs on a separate machine. A project

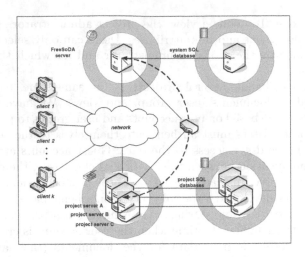

Fig. 2. Distributed FreeSoDA system topology

server may store the documents themselves, but it is possible (and often useful) to store the documents somewhere on the internet. Hence, a project server also stores information about where to actually find each document, such as a URL.

A client first contacts the central FreeSoDA server via the known URL for the FreeSoDA services. After the user has logged into the system and chosen a project to work with, the client program gets redirected by the central server to the correct project server, given that the project is hosted on a separate server. From then on, the client talks to the project server. For example, the next step is a request from the client to the project server to open one of the views onto the project.

3   Web Services

TABLE 1 lists all Web services which a user typically needs when working with a FreeSoDA database. Not all these services are allowed for all users. For example, in order to delete a document the user must be the owner of the document or a project administrator. Another example is that a user must have been granted the right to open a particular view by the project administrator.

Measures have been taken to avoid orphaned files and links. If a user deletes one of his files to which another user has set a link, the project administrator becomes the owner of the file and the link is retained. Since each link carries a type attribute and an owner attribute, links between two given documents which have been set by different users can be distinguished, as can be two links of different type created by the same user.

The client software uses the Web services offered by the FreeSoDA server to allow a user to retrieve, add, delete, and link documents in the database. Documents can be added either via a drop down menu or by dragging an existing

Table 1. Web services for working with a FreeSoDA database

service	method to be called
open a view	srvViewCtrl.RegistrationReq()
	srvViewCtrl.RegisterClient()
close a view	srvViewCtrl.DeregisterClient()
delete a document	srvViewModel.DeleteDocument()
delete a link	srvViewModel.DeleteLink()
download a document	srvViewModel.DownloadDocument()
edit a document description	srvViewModel.EditDocument()
edit a link description	srvViewModel.EditLink()
update a view	srvViewModel.GetViewUpdate()
insert a document	srvViewModel.InsertDocument()
insert a link	srvViewModel.InsertLink()
insert and link a document	srvViewModel.InsertLinkedDocument()

document onto an empty spot in the window; in the latter case, the new document will be linked with the dragged document. A link between two existing documents can be added either via the drop down menu or by dragging one document onto the other.

The client is also responsible for presenting the database to the user with a structured layout and allowing the user to traverse the database. For navigation purposes, a subset of the documents is labeled by the project administrator as the *root documents.* The screenshot below (FIGURE 3) shows a client window where the root documents are presented to the user in the left frame using a Windows Explorer-like layout. In this frame, the user can traverse the database by opening "subfolders." The right frame shows details about the currently selected document, such as its owner, creation date, and location.

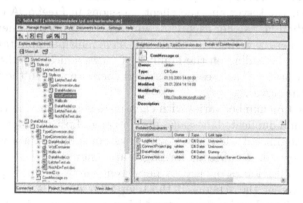

Fig. 3. Client window with Explorer-like navigation layout

Besides the Web services for handling documents and links described above, there are a number of other services which relate to managing projects and the central FreeSoDA server. These services are available only to users with project or system administrator privileges. As an example, FIGURE 4 shows the drop down menu for managing projects. Project administrators can create, edit, and delete users, assign roles to users such as being an additional project administrator, and define user groups, link types, and the filter rules for the different views which are available in the project. Similar menus are available for system-wide administration such as defining the projects and assigning administrator privileges in the FreeSoDA system.

Fig. 4. Drop down menu for managing a project

4   Messages and Sessions

A FreeSoDA server [1] and its clients exchange XML messages via the SOAP protocol. The message format implements features which are not available with SOAP and HTTP, including access rights, encryption, authentication, sessions, notifications, and a presentation layer. FIGURE 5 shows the format of a FreeSoDA XML message.

To implement the concept of sessions and transactions, each message contains a session id (`ClientGUID`) and a transaction number (`TAN`). The session id is shared between the server and the client. Sessions in FreeSoDA operate at the level of individual views: For each view which a client opens, a new session id is generated by the server. Hence, a client can have multiple simultaneous sessions with the server, depending on the number of views which have been opened by this client. The state of each session is stored (persistently) in the SQL database belonging to the server.

The transaction number varies with each message sent. Using the transaction numbers, lost and duplicated messages are detected. Lost messages are requested again after some timeout which is set by the system administrator when installing the FreeSoDA system. Duplicated messages are ignored.

Each time a session is opened, a persistent entry in the SQL database is created to represent the session. If the user later on calls a Web service, the session is re-activated and a temporary object is created inside the Web server to serve the request. This object is initialized with the data from the session entry in the SQL database. TABLE 6 shows the format of the database table for storing session objects.

The body of a FreeSoDA message holds one or more *containers*. A container not only contains the actual data, but also determines how the client should present the data to the user. Possible container types are *Edit, Insert, Select,*

---

[1] This holds for both the central server and the project servers.

```
< SoDAMessage   >
      < ClientGUID   >< / ClientGUID   >
      < Data  >
            < TAN >< / TAN >
            < Container  >                                                    { 0..n}
                  < Name  >< / Name  >
                  < Type  >< / Type  >
                  < Selectstyle   >< / Selectstyle   >
                  < Group >< / Group >                                        { 0..1}
                  < Item  >                                                   { 0..n}
                        < Key >< / Key >
                        < Value >< / Value  >
                        < Type >< / Type >
                        < Attribute  >                                        { 0..n}
                              < Name  >< / Name  >
                              < Value >< / Value  >
                              < Type  >< / Type  >
                              < Identifier   >< / Identifier   >
                              < Postback  >< / Postback  >
                        </ Attribute  >
                  < / Item  >
            < / Container  >
      </ Data >
</ SoDAMessage   >
```

Fig. 5. FreeSoDA message format

and *System*. For example, when the client reveives a message from the server asking for certain input data needed from the user in order to complete the current request, the client *generates* a suitable Web form based on the directions given in the container, presents the form to the user, and sends the data from the completed form back to the server. FIGURE 7 shows an example of such a generated Web form.

5   Event Notification Mechanism

FreeSoDA is designed to be a tool for collaboration in distributed development projects. Therefore, a central goal of the system was to make changes to the shared documentation database *immediately visible* to other users. We felt that it was not sufficient to notify users by email about recent changes to the database and ask them to refresh their display; we wanted changes to appear on the client screen automatically, given that the change is relevant to the user. This is not possible with conventional Web sites or Wiki systems. Hence, we needed to implement a full, transaction-based event notification scheme on top of our Web services.

Our event notification scheme resembles the *observer design pattern* from object-oriented programming. Each FreeSoDA view onto the document database corresponds to exactly one model in the observer pattern. The FreeSoDA clients correspond to the observers. In order to observe a model (that is, see the documents and links belonging to this FreeSoDA view), clients must register with the "controller" of the model. The controller sits inside the server. Registering and

Fig. 6. Database table for session objects

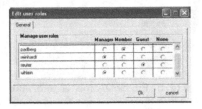

Fig. 7. A generated Web form

de-registering with a particular **FreeSoDA** view is done via Web services. Once a client has registered with a view, the controller in the server notifies the client of any changes to the database which are visible within this view. Examples of possible changes are adding or deleting a document or link. When the client gets notified of changes, it fetches a delta to its current version of the view from the server. The delta is computed in the server by comparing the *time stamp* of the client's version of the database with the current time stamp in the server.

6   Performance

Our test environment consisted of one server PC (AMD 1.1 GHz, 512 MB, Windows Server 2003) running the **FreeSoDA** server *and* the SQL database, plus several client PC (AMD 1.6 GHz, 1024 MB, Windows XP) running the client software. The PC were interconnected with a standard 100 MBit network switch. To test the performance of the **FreeSoDA** server, we requested the most expensive operation from the server: bulk updates. Bulk updates occur in practice only for freshly installed clients or when a client has been inactive for a long period of time during which the database has changed much.

First measurements showed that the server CPU quickly reaches full load during bulk updates; creating update objects is an expensive operation. To speed the server's responses up, we introduced a two-level caching scheme: We used part of the main memory as a level one cache and an additional database as a level two cache for FreeSoDA update objects. The level one cache could hold about 100 update objects, the level two cache was basically "unlimited."

The two-level caching scheme improved the performance during bulk updates with one client drastically. Given our hardware, the transmission time increased roughly linearly with the number of transmitted update objects up to about 2500 objects; the transmission time per update object was less than 8 milliseconds. Beyond 2500 objects, the transmission time increased exponentially.

Using an update window size of 500 objects, the response time of the server to an update request by the client was less than 5 seconds. This means that a user can see first progress with a larger update after 5 seconds, assuming that the client PC can display the new data fast enough. This is a good response behavior bearing in mind that bulk updates occur only rarely under real usage. Using a window size of 1000 (respectively, 2500), the response time was still less than 10 (respectively, 20) seconds.

We also studied the response times of the server when multiple clients were sending bulk update requests at the same time. Using a window size of 250, HTTP timeouts (after 90 seconds) occured for some clients when the total number of clients exceeded 8. We are currently studying how many simultaneous clients can reasonably be served assuming "normal" client requests.

A simple way to increase the performance of the FreeSoDA system is to use separate machines for the FreeSoDA server and the SQL server with a high-speed interconnect between them. In future work, we want to use server replication techniques and clustered servers to increase the performance of the system.

7 Conclusions

In this paper, we have presented FreeSoDA, a distributed and Web services-based document management system written in C# under .NET. As opposed to version control systems, FreeSoDA allows for storing and sharing documents of arbitrary type and content over the Internet, offers a mechanism for linking related files in the database (similar to hypertext systems), and implements a mechanism for notifying clients in case of changes to the database. As opposed to hypertext systems, FreeSoDA handles distributed simultaneous changes to its database and makes these changes immediately visible to all users through the notification mechanism.

From a Web technology perspective, an important novel feature of FreeSoDA is the session scheme (including authentication and encryption) which we implemented on top of SOAP. We needed sessions and transactions as a basis for controlling access to the database and implementing the notification mechanism. In our experience, the fact that Web services are *stateless* is a barrier for developing high-value applications and, hence, a clear point in favor of existing Web technologies such as EJB. Holding sessions and storing system state in a SQL database are natural requirements for middleware today, and the application developer should be freed from the burden of inventing his own scheme for that purpose when using Web services.

We currently use FreeSoDA for internal projects in our research group. A large public application on the Web is in preparation, see below. Users already ask for enhanced features, such as searching, versioning, and bookmarks.

The most challenging step when setting up a FreeSoDA database is to choose a sustainable scheme for the link types and views. This requires some foresight at the future structure and contents of the database. We shall provide sample templates once we have gained more experience with setting up large FreeSoDA systems.

FreeSoDA was originally intended as a tool which would allow the developers in an open source project to attach plain text comments to files in large source file hierarchies. The comments should be visible to all other developers in the project. The tool aimed at supporting the ROTOR [5] community. ROTOR is a shared source version of the .NET framework which is available from Microsoft as part of its Shared Source Initiative. There are more than 14,000 source files within ROTOR which are being studied extensively by universities and research groups all over the world.

We plan to host a freely accessible FreeSoDA database for ROTOR in the future. Navigation in the database will be organized along the source file hierarchy. The information contained in the already existing mailing lists will be extracted and added to the database. Research groups will get access to add other types of documentation as well, such as UML diagrams and published papers. We think that such a FreeSoDA database will help organize and push forward information exchange among the distributed research groups and will offer a major supplement to the current practice of using mailing lists.

Acknowledgements

The FreeSoDA server was written by Sven Reinhardt as part of his diploma thesis [3]. The FreeSoDA client was written by Philipp Uihlein as part of his intermediate thesis [4]. The FreeSoDA project is financially supported by Microsoft Research, Cambridge, UK.

References

1. Herbsleb and Grinter: "Splitting the Organization and Integrating the Code" Proceedings ICSE 21 (1999) 85–95
2. http://csrc.nist.gov/encryption/shs/sha256-384-512.ps
3. Reinhardt: "SoDA. Ein Webservice-basiertes verteiltes Dokumenten-Management-System" (in German), Diplomarbeit, Universität Karlsruhe, 2004
4. Uihlein: "Entwurf und Implementierung eines Clients für SoDA" (in German), Studienarbeit, Universität Karlsruhe, 2004
5. http://research.microsoft.com/programs/europe/rotor/

A JMM-Faithful Non-interference Calculus for Java

Vladimir Klebanov

University of Koblenz-Landau
Institute of Computer Science
vladimir@uni-koblenz.de

Abstract. We present a calculus for establishing non-interference of several Java threads running in parallel. The proof system is built atop an implemented sequential Java Dynamic Logic calculus with 100% Java Card coverage. We present two semantic and one syntactic type of non-interference conditions to make reasoning efficient. In contrast to previous works in this direction, our method takes into full account the weak guarantees of the Java Memory Model concerning visibility and ordering of memory updates between threads.

1 Introduction

Concurrent programming in Java, as in other languages supporting concurrency and shared memory, exposes the phenomenon of *interference*. Sequential programs proven correct may go awry when composed as threads in a concurrent setting. The problem results from concurrent modification of shared datastructures, and its control has been long of interest in software verification (albeit mostly for simple programming languages).

We present a proof system for establishing non-interference of Java threads, i.e., we specify the conditions $\Phi_1 \ldots \Phi_n$ such that the following parallel composition rule (stated using dynamic logic) is sound.

$$\frac{\langle p_1\rangle\phi_1 \quad \langle p_2\rangle\phi_2 \quad \Phi_1 \ldots \Phi_n}{\langle p_1 \parallel p_2\rangle\phi_1 \wedge \phi_2} \text{ PAR\_COMP}$$

In contrast to previous works in this field [1], our proof system takes into full account the weak guarantees of the Java Memory Model (JMM) concerning visibility and ordering of memory updates between threads. Software verified with our method will thus always work as expected when executed on a real Java Virtual Machine.

The calculus we present follows the style of Owicki and Gries [9]. While the Owicki-Gries method is not compositional, we have chosen this fundamental approach for our work before working on compositionality. Also, only the mutual exclusion primitives of Java (the `synchronized` keyword) are considered. Primitives for condition synchronization (`wait()` and `notify()`) are not.

Our work is based on an implemented and complete sequential proof system – the KeY system [7, 2] – which we will introduce briefly.

N. Guelfi et al. (Eds.): FIDJI 2004, LNCS 3409, pp. 101–111, 2005.

2   Foundations

2.1   Java Dynamic Logic

Introduced in [3], Java Dynamic Logic (Java DL) is a modal logic with the modalities $\langle p \rangle$ ("diamond") and $[p]$ ("box") for every program p. The modality $\langle p \rangle$ refers to the successor worlds (called states in the DL framework) that are reachable by running the program p. The formula $\langle p \rangle \phi$ expresses that the program p terminates in a state, in which ϕ holds. In contrast, the formula $[p]\phi$ asserts that, if the program p terminates, then in a state satisfying ϕ.

A formula $\phi \rightarrow \langle p \rangle \psi$ is valid if, for every state s satisfying precondition ϕ, a run of the program p starting in s terminates, and in the terminating state the post-condition ψ holds. Thus, the formula $\phi \rightarrow [p]\psi$ is similar to the Hoare triple $\{\phi\}p\{\psi\}$, while $\phi \rightarrow \langle p \rangle \psi$ implies the total correctness of p.

2.2   The KeY Calculus

As usual for deductive program verification, we use a sequent-style calculus. A *sequent* is of the form $\Gamma \vdash \Delta$, where Γ, Δ are duplicate-free lists of formulas. Intuitively, its semantics is the same as that of the formula $\bigwedge \Gamma \rightarrow \bigvee \Delta$.

A *proof* for a goal (a sequent) S is an upside-down tree with root S. In practice, rules are applied from bottom to top. That is, proof construction starts with the initial proof obligation at the bottom and ends with axioms (rules with an empty premiss tuple).

Besides the standard first-order and rewriting rules, the KeY calculus contains rules for symbolic execution of Java programs and induction. Most rules (rule instances) have a *focus*, i.e., a single formula, term, or program part (in the conclusion of the rule) that is modified or deleted by applying the rule.

Furthermore, symbolic execution rules operate only on the first *active* statement p of a program $\pi p \omega$. The non-active prefix π consists of an arbitrary sequence of opening braces "{", labels, beginnings "try{" of try-catch-finally blocks, etc. The postfix ω denotes the "rest" of the program. For example, if a rule is applied to the following Java block, the active statement is i=0;:

$$\underbrace{\texttt{l:\{try\{}}_{\pi} \; \texttt{i=0;} \; \underbrace{\texttt{j=0; \}finally\{ k=0; \}\}.}}_{\omega}$$

Since there is (at least) one rule schema in the Java DL calculus for each Java programming construct, we cannot present all of them in this paper. Instead, we give a simple but typical example, the rule IF_ELSE_SPLIT for the if statement:

$$\frac{\Gamma, \; b = \text{TRUE} \;\vdash\; \langle \pi \; p \; \omega \rangle \phi \qquad \Gamma, \; b = \text{FALSE} \;\vdash\; \langle \pi \; q \; \omega \rangle \phi}{\Gamma \;\vdash\; \langle \pi \; \texttt{if}(b) \; p \; \texttt{else} \; q \; \omega \rangle \phi} \quad \text{IF\_ELSE\_SPLIT}$$

The rule has two premisses, which correspond to the two cases of the if statement. The semantics of this rule is that, if the two premisses hold in a state, then the conclusion is true in that state. In particular, if the two premisses are valid, then the conclusion is valid. Note, that this rule is only applicable if the condition b is known (syntactically) to be free of side-effect. Otherwise, if b is a complex expression, other rules have to be applied first to evaluate b.

2.3 Symbolic Execution

We will call an application of a rule that has a program as its focus (e.g., IF_ELSE_SPLIT) a *symbolic execution step*. Each symbolic execution step is thus inherently related to (1) a sequent (matching the conclusion of the rule), (2) a modal formula in this sequent, (3) the program in this formula, and (4) the active (first) statement in this program.

To unify the presentation, we assume that the focus sequent of every symbolic execution step is of the form

$$\Gamma \vdash \mathcal{U}\langle p\rangle\phi \quad \text{or} \quad \Gamma \vdash \mathcal{U}[p]\phi$$

where $\mathcal{U}$ is a (possibly empty) list of updates, which are described below. This requirement does not destroy completeness and can be easily achieved by inserting first-order normalization steps into any given proof. In the following we will use the sequent form with a diamond; the results are valid for the box form as well though.

2.4 Updates

A special significance comes to the assignment rules(s) when handling program state. The Java Dynamic Logic does not work with states as first-class citizens. Assignment cannot be treated by syntactic substitution either because of aliasing (the possibility that different syntactical entities reference the same storage location). The solution Java DL employs is called *updates*.

These (state) updates are of the form $\langle loc := se\rangle$ and can be put in front of any formula or term. This expression then has to be evaluated in the state where loc has the value se. The expressions loc and se must be simple in the following sense: loc is (a) a local variable var, or (b) a field access obj.attr, or (c) an array access arr[i]; and se is free of side effects. More complex expressions are not allowed in updates. Other rules have to be applied first to break these down.

The assignment rule takes the following form ($\mathcal{U}$ stands for an arbitrary sequence of updates):

$$\frac{\Gamma \vdash \mathcal{U}\langle loc := se\rangle\langle \pi\ \omega\rangle\phi}{\Gamma \vdash \mathcal{U}\langle \pi\ loc\ =\ se;\ \omega\rangle\phi} \text{ ASSIGNMENT}$$

That is, it just adds the assignment to the list of updates $\mathcal{U}$. The KeY system uses special simplification rules to compute the result of applying an update to logical terms and formulas not containing programs. This delayed evaluation has the advantage that a maximal amount of information is available for efficient simplification after the program has been symbolically executed to completion.

3   Characterizing Program State with Formulas

To reason about (non-)interference of symbolic execution steps we need to make tangible the notion of program state, which the KeY calculus never handles explicitly. All sequents are evaluated in the same (start) state; evaluation of individual formulas can be performed in a changed state by attachment of updates.

Definition 1 (Sequent state formula $state(S)$) By restricting the focus sequent form as described above, we define a single formula characterizing the program state in which a given symbolic execution step originates. For a sequent S of the form $\Gamma \vdash \langle x := y \rangle \langle p \rangle \phi$

$$state(S) := \exists v \langle x := v \rangle \Gamma \wedge x \doteq \langle x := v \rangle y$$

where Γ in this formula is a conjunction of all formulas in the antecedent of the sequent S.

Note. The above definition is simplified for the assumption that there is only one update and x is unqualified. If x is of the form $o.a$ then the second conjunct must read $(\langle x := v \rangle o).a \doteq \langle x := v \rangle y$. If x is of the form $a[i]$ then the second conjunct must read $(\langle x := v \rangle a)[\langle x := v \rangle i] \doteq \langle x := v \rangle y$. The extension for several updates is straightforward.   ◁

The definition given above encodes information about the state contained in Γ and the updates attached to $\langle p \rangle \phi$ as a single formula of our logic. The fresh variable v is used to capture the value of x prior to performing the update. An example is presented in Table 1.

Table 1. Example for state characterization

Sequent S	$state(S)$	Validity Eqv.
$x \doteq 0 \vdash \langle x := x + 1 \rangle \langle p \rangle \phi$	$\exists v \langle x := v \rangle x \doteq 0 \wedge x \doteq \langle x := v \rangle x + 1$	$x \doteq 1$
$x \doteq 0 \vdash \langle x := 2 \rangle \langle p \rangle \phi$	$\exists v \langle x := v \rangle x \doteq 0 \wedge x \doteq \langle x := v \rangle 2$	$x \doteq 2$

Theorem 1 (State characterization is adequate)   The sequent S of the form $\Gamma \vdash \langle x := y \rangle \langle p \rangle \phi$ and the sequent $\vdash state(S) \rightarrow \langle p \rangle \phi$ are validity equivalent.   ◁

4   Semantic Non-interference Conditions

A proof tree for a property of a single sequential program represents all possible paths of program execution steps. We wish to ascertain that each of these steps can be performed correctly (w.r.t. our desired property) even if the scheduler chooses to interleave steps from other threads that are running in parallel. In other words, we verify that the assumptions required for the correctness proof of one thread are not damaged by the updates that other threads might carry out on the common state.

Definition 2 (Proof robustness) A proof P_1 is *robust* under parallel composition with proof P_2 if for every symbolic execution step S_1 in P_1 and every symbolic execution step S_2 in P_2 that performs a state update the condition $\Phi(S_1, S_2)$ holds. Different kinds of the condition Φ are presented below.   ◁

Now we employ the notion of proof robustness to state the main result of symmetric non-interference.

Theorem 2 (Non-Interference) Two proofs P_1 and P_2 are *non-interfering* if P_1 is robust under parallel composition with P_2, and P_2 is robust under parallel composition with P_1. The parallel composition rule PAR_COMP is correct with these premises. A justification is presented in Section 4.3.   ◁

Thus, to establish non-interference involving two threads with m and n statements we have to verify $O(m \times n)$ conditions. For this reason it is desirable that the conditions are as simple as possible. The majority of these conditions can, in fact, be discharged automatically. In the following we present and discuss two semantic and one syntactic condition.

Note on Inter- vs. Intra-object Interference. The number of noninterference conditions can be reduced dramatically up-front if we prohibit qualified access to fields in programs (as in [1]). Under this (sensible) restriction, expressions like $o.a$ are not allowed, and methods can only refer to fields of the local object, like $this.a$. Interference is thus confined within object boundaries, which allows us to drop all conditions that involve code from classes not in a direct line of inheritance.

Note on Double and Long Variables. The semantical conditions rely on the atomicity of a simple assignment in the sense of Section 2.4. This atomicity is not given for variables declared as `double` or `long` [8, §8.4].

4.1   Preservation of Pre-state

A Naive Version. We will start with a simplified version of $\Phi(S_1, S_2)$, which is analogous to previous formulations of the Owicki-Gries method. This simplification assumes the existence of a consistent global state for both threads. It is adequate for theoretical programming languages or a Java VM with much stronger memory model guarantees than the ones actually given by the current official specification. We will weaken these assumptions later on.

The now following condition ensures that the execution of an (atomic) assignment $loc{=}se$; in the sequent of S_2 does not falsify assumptions appearing in the symbolic execution step with sequent S_1. The condition $\Phi(S_1, S_2)$ is expressed in this case by a logical formula, which has to be proved in our calculus.

We define

$$\Phi_{\mathrm{pre}}(S_1, S_2) := state(S_1) \land state(S_2) \rightarrow [loc\texttt{=}se\,;\,]state(S_1)$$

Note the use of the box modality here, since $loc\texttt{=}se$; could terminate abruptly due to a `NullPointerException` (if loc is a field or array access) or an `ArrayIndex-OutOfBoundsException` (if loc is an array access). In case of abrupt termination no state update is performed, and there is no danger of interference, as the thrown exception is not visible to other threads. A diamond modality would, in contrast, always require normal termination.

A JMM-Faithful Version. For a single thread the JMM provides strong guarantees about the visibility and ordering of memory updates, which are consistent with our intuition and reflected by the KeY calculus [8, § 8.1]. There is, however, no guarantee that memory updates performed by one thread will be visible (in any particular order, or even at all) by other threads in absence of proper synchronization [8, §§8.1, 8.3, 8.11].

Example 1 Let x, y be object fields. With naive semantics in mind, one could believe the proof for $\langle \texttt{y=2;x=2;}\rangle x \doteq 2$ to be robust under execution of the assignment $\texttt{x=y;}$ in a second thread. The crucial condition required to prove this is (we simplify the state characterizations)

$$x \doteq 2 \land y \doteq 2 \rightarrow [\texttt{x=y;}]x \doteq 2$$

which obviously holds. In the JMM-faithful semantics this robustness, however, cannot be expected. The effect of the assignment $\texttt{y=2;}$ may be not visible for the thread number two, and the assignment $\texttt{x=y;}$ (scheduled after $\texttt{x=2;}$) would operate with a stale value of y, which is not necessarily 2.

To reflect the fact that we cannot rely on updates performed by other threads, we have to establish variable disjointness by renaming variables in one of the threads. This turns the condition above into

$$x \doteq 2 \land y \doteq 2 \rightarrow [\texttt{x=y';}]x \doteq 2$$

which (correctly) cannot be proved.   ◁

The condition Φ_{pre} has thus to be recast as Φ'_{pre}:

$$\Phi'_{\mathrm{pre}}(S_1, S_2) := state(S_1) \land state'(S_2) \rightarrow [loc\texttt{=}se'\,;\,]state(S_1)$$

where $state'(S_2)$ differs from $state(S_2)$ in that all appearing object fields have been renamed (accented by a dash). se' appears in that manner in the place of se in the assignment in the box. This version of the condition is significantly stronger, as no information flow is assumed from the first thread to the second. Since the JMM does not guarantee memory update visibility between threads (in absence of proper synchronization) such an assumption would be indeed false.

On the other hand, should the update `loc=se'`; not become visible to the first thread, we would have solely proved one condition too many, thus erring on the safe side.

Note on Volatile Variables. A relaxation of the above condition can be achieved for variables declared as `volatile`. For volatile variables the JMM enforces state coherence, i.e., the value of a volatile variable is always visible correctly across all threads. Volatile variables thus need not be accented with a dash in Φ'_{pre}.

4.2 Assertion Insensitivity

Failing to prove a Φ_{pre} condition does not necessarily mean interference. Non-interference could still be established by considering a more general condition at this point. This time the assignment loc=se; in the sequent S_2 is allowed to falsify assumptions made in S_1, but only if this does not affect the provability of the main assertion of S_1. We define

$$\Phi_{\text{post}}(S_1, S_2) := state(S_1) \wedge state'(S_2) \rightarrow [loc\text{=}se'\,;]\langle p\rangle\phi$$

Such a criterion is more powerful but less practical, as it involves proving a version of the (complicated) assertion $\langle p\rangle\phi$. Furthermore, this proof has to be checked (with the usual criteria) for non-interference too.

4.3 Correctness of the Parallel Composition Rule

We give a general proof-theoretical argument for the correctness of the composition rule from Section 1 under the specified non-interference conditions, concentrating on the Φ_{pre} case. Details for other condition types can be found in the corresponding sections. An important prerequisite for the argument is the completeness of the KeY calculus w.r.t. the Java Dynamic Logic[1]: we assume that there is a proof for every true assertion in the sequential fragment.

In the following, we will present and justify a transformation that allows (under conditions specified above) to derive a proof for $\langle p_1 \| p_2\rangle\phi_1$ from the proof for $\langle p_1\rangle\phi_1$ alone. Since the situation is symmetrical, we can derive that $\langle p_1 \| p_2\rangle\phi_2$ holds whenever $\langle p_2\rangle\phi_2$ holds, and thus establish $\langle p_1 \| p_2\rangle\phi_1 \wedge \phi_2$.

Every proof step in a proof falls into one of the following categories:

- **Proof steps without modality in focus.** These rules are in the "propositional" fragment. It is thus safe to replace every modality of the form $\langle p\rangle$ in the conclusion and premises of this step with $\langle p \| p_2\rangle$.
- **Update simplification steps.** Update simplification rules have no dependency on the modality they are attached to. The same replacement can be performed.

---

[1] Efforts are currently underway to provide a formal completeness proof [10].

– **Symbolic execution steps.** Every symbolic execution step establishes the validity of the sequent $S_1 : \Gamma \vdash U \langle p \rangle \phi_1$. A single non-interference condition $\Phi(S_1, S_2)$ states that starting in any state that satisfies $state(S_1)$ and executing an assignment from the program p_2 running in parallel, we arrive in a state that still satisfies $state(S_1)$ (it need not be the same state). The same is true of any sequence of such assignments, or finally the whole program p_2. Thus we can replace every occurrence of the formula $\langle p \rangle \phi$ in the focus of a symbolic execution step with the formula $\langle p \| p_2 \rangle \phi$ without sacrificing the correctness of the proof.

5 Syntactic Non-interference Condition

This type of condition is less powerful than the two discussed above, but allows in many cases to dismiss the possibility of interference immediately and without interaction. Informally, syntactical non-interference is given if programs deal with disjoint memory locations if write access is involved. We will identify a read set and a write set for every rule of our calculus denoting symbolic memory locations read resp. written by the corresponding symbolic execution step.

Definition 3 (Write Set $W(r)$) The *write set* contains symbolic locations whose content is changed by a symbolic execution rule. The only rule with a non-empty write set is the ASSIGNMENT rule:

$$\frac{\Gamma \vdash U \langle loc := se \rangle \langle \pi \ \omega \rangle \phi}{\Gamma \vdash U \langle \pi \ loc = se; \ \omega \rangle \phi} \ \text{ASSIGNMENT}$$

We define $W = loc$, if loc is not a local variable.   ◁

Definition 4 (Read Set $R(r)$) An expression e contained in the read set of a rule r is characterized by the following conditions:

1. e appears inside the diamond in the conclusion of r (i.e., the focus of r)
2. e appears outside a diamond in the premisses of r (including updates, though not on the left-hand side)
3. e is not a local variable   ◁

Example 2

– Assuming se is not a local variable, $R(\text{ASSIGNMENT}) = \{se\}$ as se appears in the focus diamond of the conclusion and outside of it in the premiss. $loc \notin R(\text{ASSIGNMENT})$ since it appears on the left-hand side of an update. On the other hand $loc \in W(\text{ASSIGNMENT})$.
– $R(\text{IF\_ELSE\_SPLIT}) = \{b\}$, again, assuming b is not a local variable.
– Consider the rule IF_ELSE_EVAL

$$\frac{\Gamma \vdash \langle \pi \ \text{boolean} \ b; \ b=nse; \ \text{if}(nse) \ p \ \text{else} \ q \ \omega \rangle \phi}{\Gamma \vdash \langle \pi \ \text{if}(nse) \ p \ \text{else} \ q \ \omega \rangle \phi} \ \text{IF\_ELSE\_EVAL}$$

$R(\text{IF\_ELSE\_EVAL}) = \emptyset$ as this rule replaces one diamond through another with the same transition relation. There is no state change and no change in observable conditions. Note that there is a subtle issue at stake here in that the symbolic execution rules do not "swallow" any state transitions. Replacing i++;i--; with an empty statement is not allowed.   ◁

Definition 5 (Syntactic Non-interference) Within the framework of Theorem 2 we define a syntactical non-interference condition $\Phi_{\text{synt}}(S_1, S_2)$. For this we need to consider the rules r_1 and r_2 involved in the steps S_1 and S_2. We define that $\Phi_{\text{synt}}(S_1, S_2)$ holds if and only if

$$R_{S_1}(r_1) \sqcap W_{S_2}(r_2) = \emptyset$$
$$W_{S_1}(r_1) \sqcap R_{S_2}(r_2) = \emptyset$$
$$W_{S_1}(r_1) \sqcap W_{S_2}(r_2) = \emptyset$$

where $\sqcap$ denotes intersection under aliasing.   ◁

Intersection under aliasing treats two symbolic locations as the same if – regardless of their syntactical form – there is a possibility that they are referring to the same effective location due to aliasing. Since we have excluded local variables up front, we can safely assume two symbolic locations as distinct under aliasing only if they are of non-compatible types.

Ultimately, $\Phi_{\text{synt}}(S_1, S_2)$ ensures that program behavior does not change in presence of other programs. It can be used in place of $\Phi'_{\text{pre}}(S_1, S_2)$ until the "last" symbolic execution is reached (i.e., S_1 removes an empty modality). At this point, the intactness of the first-order assertions must be checked with $\Phi'_{\text{pre}}(S_1, S_2)$.

6 Synchronization

A special concurrency primitive of Java is the **synchronized** keyword. This primitive can be used to achieve mutual exclusion of critical code sections. Blocks of code or whole methods can be declared as synchronized. Synchronization happens with respect to an object being locked (for synchronized methods it is always the current object).

The semantics of synchronized is that no two distinct threads can concurrently execute code marked as synchronized w.r.t. the same lockable object reference. One of the threads would block at the attempt to acquire the lock already held by the other thread. Note that mutual exclusion does not take place if only one code section is declared as synchronized (synchronization is not atomicity), or if the lock object references of two synchronized code sections are different.

This leads us to the following refinement of our semantic conditions. If the statement in focus of the symbolic execution step S_1 as well as the assignment in focus of S_2 both lie within a code section marked as synchronized, and the statement of S_1 is not the first statement in the section, we can relax the non-interference condition Φ'_{pre} to:

$$\Phi'_{\text{pre}(s)}(S_1, S_2) := state(S_1) \wedge state'(S_2) \wedge \neg syncref(S_1) \doteq syncref(S_2) \rightarrow$$
$$[loc=se';]state(S_1)$$

where $syncref(S_1)$ and $syncref(S_2)$ are the lock references of the two sections. If these references are the same, the non-interference condition holds automatically since the JVM guarantees mutual exclusion.

Synchronization and Memory Update Visibility. The `synchronized` keyword has also a second meaning in Java. Beside mutual exclusion functions, it has a signaling function to the JVM memory subsystem. When a thread exits a synchronized code section, the content of its local store is flushed into the main memory. An entry into a synchronized code section, on the other hand, effects a reloading of the main memory content into the thread's working store [8, §8.6].

An immediate succession of these two events is thus a means for one thread to obtain a complete and consistent visibility of memory updates performed by another thread. Unfortunately, tracking such *rendez-vous* requires considering complete concurrency histories, which is is outside of the scope of a non-interference calculus.

7 Conclusion, Comparison and Future Work

We have presented (to our knowledge) the first non-interference proof system for the Java language, which reflects the actual execution semantics as stated by the Java Virtual Machine specification. Among related works, [1] does not take the JMM into account, while [4] gives a JMM-faithful operational semantics but does not provide a proof system. Furthermore, our proof system is built atop an implemented, complete calculus for sequential Java. A prototype implementation of it is available with the latest version of the KeY system.

It remains to be seen how the compositional extensions to the Owicki-Gries method, e.g., [5, 11], can be made to work in the JMM-constrained situation. Changes would also probably be necessary if the Java Memory Model revision effort [6] is successful. Development of more powerful parallel composition rules is furthermore of interest.

Acknowledgment

I wish to thank Bernhard Beckert for fruitful discussions, and Christoph Gladisch and Anne Tretow for their help with the implementation.

References

1. Erika Ábrahám, Frank S. de Boer, Willem-Paul de Roever, and Martin Steffen. Inductive proof-outlines for monitors in Java. In *International Conference on Formal Methods for Open Object-based Distributed Systems (FMOODS)*, 2003. A longer version appeared as Software Technologie technical report TR-ST-03-1, April 2003.
2. Wolfgang Ahrendt, Thomas Baar, Bernhard Beckert, Richard Bubel, Martin Giese, Reiner Hähnle, Wolfram Menzel, Wojciech Mostowski, Andreas Roth, Steffen Schlager, and Peter H. Schmitt. The KeY tool. *Software and System Modeling (SoSysM)*, pages 1–42, 2004. Available at http://www.springerlink.com.

3. Bernhard Beckert. A dynamic logic for the formal verification of Java Card programs. In I. Attali and T. Jensen, editors, *Java on Smart Cards: Programming and Security. Revised Papers, Java Card 2000, International Workshop, Cannes, France*, LNCS 2041, pages 6–24. Springer, 2001.
4. Pietro Cenciarelli, Alexander Knapp, Bernhard Reus, and Martin Wirsing. An event-based structural operational semantics of multi-threaded Java. In *Formal Syntax and Semantics of Java*, pages 157–200. Springer-Verlag, 1999.
5. Cliff B. Jones. *Development methods for computer programs including a notion of interference*. PhD thesis, Oxford University, 1981.
6. Java memory model and thread specification revision. Website at http://jcp.org/en/jsr/detail?id=133.
7. KeY Project. Website at www.key-project.org.
8. T. Lindholm and F. Yellin. *The Java Virtual Machine Specification*. Addison-Wesley, 1996.
9. S. Owicki and D. Gries. Verifying properties of parallel programs: an axiomatic approach. *Communications of the ACM*, 19(5):279–285, May 1976.
10. André Platzer. An object-oriented dynamic logic with updates. Master's thesis, Universität Karlsruhe, 2004.
11. C. Stirling. A generalization of Owicki-Gries's Hoare logic for a concurrent while language. *Theoretical Computer Science*, 58:347–359, 1988.

A Java Package for Transparent Code Mobility*

Lorenzo Bettini

Dipartimento di Sistemi e Informatica, Università di Firenze
Via Lombroso 6/17, 50134 Firenze, Italy
bettini@dsi.unifi.it

Abstract. We describe the architecture and the implementation of a Java package for code mobility. The framework aims at providing the programmer with primitives to design and implement run-time systems for mobile code systems and languages. The package is intended to be straightforward to use and to make the code migration issue automatic and transparent so that mobile agent systems can be easily prototyped. With this respect the package is general and does not depend on any linguistic mobile code abstraction.

1 Introduction

Dealing with *code mobility* requires additional programming for packing and delivering of objects state and code. With this respect, Java [2] provides many useful features that are helpful in building network applications with mobile code: *object serialization*, to encode/decode object structure into/from a stream; *dynamic class loading*, to insert a new class dynamically into a running application. However, these mechanisms still require a big programming effort, and so they can be thought of as "low-level" mechanisms. Because of this, many existing Java based distributed systems (see, e.g., [10, 1, 12, 7, 5, 14] and the references therein) tend to re-implement from scratch many components (in particular code mobility handling) that are typical and recurrent in distributed and mobile applications.

For this reason we are working on a generic framework called IMC (*Implementing Mobile Calculi*) that can be used as a kind of middleware for the implementation of different mobile programming systems. Such a framework aims at being as general as possible. We are using it to re-design existing systems (KLAVA [6], Safe Ambients [16], JCL [8] and DiTyCO [11]) on top of it. But it also provides the necessary tools for implementing new languages directly derived from calculi for mobility. The basic idea and motivation of this framework is that the implementer of a new language would need concentrating on the parts that are really specific of his system, while relying on the framework for the recurrent standard mechanisms. The development of prototype implementations should then be quicker and the programmers should be relieved from dealing with low level details.

The proposed middleware framework aims at providing all the required functionalities and abstractions (such as, network topology, communication protocols, code mobility, etc.) for arbitrary components to communicate and move in a distributed setting.

* This work has been funded by EU-FET on Global Computing, project MIKADO IST-2001-32222. The funding body is not responsible for any use that might be made of the results presented here.

N. Guelfi et al. (Eds.): FIDJI 2004, LNCS 3409, pp. 112–122, 2005.

A first presentation of the IMC framework can be found in [4]. In this paper we concentrate on the description of the mobility code part of the framework. Indeed, this part can be used independently from the other classes of the IMC framework. The purpose of this package for code mobility is to provide the basic functionalities for making code mobility transparent to the programmer; all issues related to code marshaling and code dispatch are handled automatically by the classes of the framework. Its components are designed to deal with object marshalling, code migration, and dynamic loading of code. Customization of the framework can be achieved seamlessly thanks to design patterns such as *factory method* and *abstract factory* [9] that are widely used throughout the package.

Indeed, the primary goal of our package is to make code mobility straightforward to use (as shown in Section 3, using the package to achieve code mobility in a distributed framework requires only few lines of code). In very many ways, this is the distinguishing feature of our approach with respect to other mobility frameworks such as, e.g., μCODE [13], where the main intention is to provide the programmer with a finer-grain control on class mobility. Moreover, our mobility package is more general purpose with respect to the *Aglets* [10] framework that, being centered on mobile agents, require the user of the framework to strictly conform to the rules of the framework itself.

2 The mobility **Package**

We describe the basic functionalities for code mobility provided by our package org.mikado.imc.mobility (referred to as mobility from now on). We will go into details of some parts of the package in order to describe its architecture. However, let us stress that the user of the package needs not know all these details: as shown in Section 3, the steps to use the package are minimal, although some parts are still open to possible customizations. This package defines the basic abstractions for code marshalling and unmarshalling and also implements the classes for handling Java byte-code mobility transparently. The package, together with the whole IMC framework, is freely available at http://music.dsi.unifi.it/software.

The base classes and the interfaces of this package abstract away from the low level details of the code that migrates. By redefining specific classes of the package, the framework can be adapted to deal with different code mobility frameworks. Nowadays, most of these frameworks actually exchange Java byte-code itself. For this reason, the concrete classes of the framework deal with Java byte-code mobility, and provide functionalities that can be already used, without interventions, to build the code mobility part of a Java-based code mobility framework.

When code (e.g., a process or an object) is moved to a remote computer, its classes may be unknown at the destination site. It might then be necessary to make such code available for execution at remote hosts; this can be done basically in two different ways: *automatic* approach, i.e., the classes needed by the moved process are collected and delivered together with the process; *on-demand* approach, i.e., the class needed by the remote computer that received a process for execution is requested to the server that did send the process. We follow the automatic approach because it complies better with the mobile agent paradigm: when migrating, an agent takes with it all the information that it may need for later executions. This approach respects the main aim of this package, i.e., it makes the code migration details completely transparent to the programmer, so that he will not have to worry about classes movement. The drawback of this approach is that code that may never be used by the mobile agent or that is already provided by the remote site is also shipped; for this reason we also enable the programmer to choose whether this automatic code collection and dispatching should be enabled.

With the automatic approach, an object will be sent along with its class binary code, and with the class code of all the objects it uses. Obviously, only the code of user defined classes has to be sent, as the other code (e.g. Java class libraries and the classes of the mobility package itself) has to be common to every application. This guarantees that classes belonging to Java standard class libraries are not loaded from other sources (especially, the network); this would be very dangerous, since, in general, such classes have many more access privileges with respect to other classes.

2.1 Design of the Package

The package defines the empty interface MigratingCode that must be implemented by the classes representing a code that has to be exchanged among distributed site. This code is intended to be transmitted in a MigratingPacket, stored in the shape of a byte array:

```
public class MigratingPacket implements java.io.Serializable {
    public MigratingPacket(byte[] b) {...}
    public byte[] getObjectBytes() {...}
}
```

How a MigratingCode object is stored in and retrieved from a MigratingPacket is taken care of by the these two interfaces:

```
public interface MigratingCodeMarshaller {
    MigratingPacket marshal(MigratingCode code) throws IOException;
}
```

```
public interface MigratingCodeUnMarshaller {
    MigratingCode unmarshal(MigratingPacket p)
     throws InstantiationException, IllegalAccessException, ClassNotFoundException,
        IOException;
}
```

Starting from these interfaces, the package mobility provides concrete classes that automatically deal with migration of Java objects together with their byte-code, and for transparently deserializing such objects by dynamically loading their transmitted byte-code. These classes are described in the following. A simplified UML diagrams of the main classes of the package is depicted in Figure 1.

2.2 Java Byte-Code Mobility

All the nodes that are willing to accept code from remote sites must have a custom *class loader*: a NodeClassLoader supplied by the mobility package. When a remote object or a migrating process is received from the network, before using it, the node must add the class binary data (received along with the object) to its class loader's

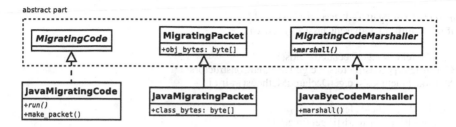

Fig. 1. Main classes in the package.

table. Then, during the execution, whenever a class code is needed, if the class loader does not find the code in the local packages, then it can find it in its own local table of class binary data. The most important methods that concern a node willing to accept code from remote sites are addClassBytes to update the loader's class table, as said above, and forceLoadClass to bootstrap the class loader mechanism, as explained later:

```
public class NodeClassLoader extends java.lang.ClassLoader {
  public void addClassBytes(String className, byte[] classBytes) {...}
  public Class forceLoadClass(String className) {...}
}
```

We define a base class for all objects/processes that can migrate to a remote site, JavaMigratingCode, implementing the above mentioned interface, MigratingCode, that provides all the procedures for collecting the Java classes that the migrating object has to bring to the remote site. Unfortunately, Java only provides single inheritance, thus providing a base class might restrict its usability. The problem arises when dealing with threads: the interface Runnable in the standard Java class library could solve the above issue but requires additional programming. For this reason we make JavaMigratingCode a subclass of java.lang.Thread (with an empty run method), so that JavaMigratingCode can be extended easily by classes that are meant to be threads. Thus, the most relevant methods for the programmer are the following ones:

```
public class JavaMigratingCode extends Thread implements MigratingCode {
  public void run() { /* empty */ }
  public JavaMigratingPacket make_packet() throws IOException {...}
}
```

The programmer will redefine run if its class is intended to represent a thread. The method make_packet will be used directly by the other classes of the framework or, possibly, directly by the programmer, to build a packet containing the serialized (marshalled) version of the object that has to migrate together with all its needed byte code. Thus, this method will actually take care of all the code collection operations. The names of user defined classes can be retrieved by means of class introspection (*Java Reflection API*). Just before dispatching a process to a remote site, a recursive procedure is called for collecting all classes that are used by the process when declaring: data members, objects returned by or passed to a method/constructor, exceptions thrown by methods, inner classes, the interfaces implemented by its class, the base class of

```
protected void getUsedClasses( Class c ) {
  if (c == null || ! addUsedClass( c )) return ;

  Field[] fields = c.getDeclaredFields() ;
  Constructor[] constructors = c.getDeclaredConstructors() ;
  Method[] methods = c.getDeclaredMethods() ; int i ;

  for( i = 0 ; i < fields.length ; i++ )
    getUsedClasses( fields[i].getType() ) ;

  for ( i = 0 ; i < constructors.length ; i++ ) {
    getUsedClasses( constructors[i].getParameterTypes() ) ;
    getUsedClasses( constructors[i].getExceptionTypes() ) ;
  }

  for ( i = 0 ; i < methods.length; i++ ) {
    getUsedClasses( methods[i].getReturnType() ) ;
    getUsedClasses( methods[i].getParameterTypes() ) ;
    getUsedClasses( methods[i].getExceptionTypes() ) ;
  }

  getUsedClasses( c.getDeclaredClasses() ) ;
  getUsedClasses( c.getSuperclass() ) ;
  getUsedClasses( c.getInterfaces() ) ;
}
```

Listing 1. The methods to collect the classes used by a `MigratingCode` object through reflection. The version taking an array simply iterates on the elements.

its class. These operations are performed internally by the method `getUsedClasses`, displayed in Listing 1.

Once these class names are collected, their byte code is gathered in the first server from which the object was sent, and packed along with the object in a `JavaMigratingPacket` object (a subclass of `MigratingPacket` storing the byte-code of all the classes used by the migrating object, besides the serialized object itself). Notice that the migrating object (namely, its variables) is written in an array of bytes (inherited by `MigratingPacket`) and not in a field of type `JavaMigratingCode`. This is necessary because otherwise, when the packet is received at the remote site and read from the stream, the remote object would be deserialized and an error would be raised when any of its specific classes is needed (indeed, the class is in the packet but has not yet been read). Instead, by using our representation, we have that, first, the byte code of process classes is read from the packet and stored in the class loader table of the receiving node; then, the object is read from the byte array; when its classes are needed, the class loader finds them in its own table. Thus, when a node receives a process, after filling in the class loader's table, it simply deserialize the process, without any need of explicit instantiation. The point here is that classes are always stored in the class loader's table, but they are loaded on-demand.

The byte code of the classes used by a migrating process or object is retrieved by the method `getClassBytes` of the class loader: at the server from where the object is first sent, the byte code is retrieved from the local file system, but when a process at a remote site has to be sent to another remote site, the byte code for its classes is obtained from the class loader's table of the node.

Finally, two classes, implementing the above mentioned interfaces `Migrating-CodeMarshaller` and `MigratingCodeUnMarshaller`, will take care of actually marshalling and unmarshalling a `JavaMigratingPacket` containing a migrating object and its code:

public class JavaByteCodeMarshaller **implements** MigratingCodeMarshaller {...}
public class JavaByteCodeUnMarshaller **implements** MigratingCodeUnMarshaller {...}

In particular, the first one will basically rely on the method `make_packet` of `JavaMigratingCode`, while the second one will rely on `NodeClassLoader` to load the classes stored in the `JavaMigratingPacket` and then on Java serialization to actually deserialize the migrating code contained in the packet.

Now let us examine the code that recovers the object from a `JavaMigrating-Packet`, in the `JavaByteCodeUnMarshaller`. As previously hinted, a site that is willing to receive a remote object must use a `NodeClassLoader` that will take care of loading the classes received with a `JavaMigratingPacket`. The Java class loading strategy works as follows: whenever a class A is needed during the execution of a program, if it is not already loaded, then the class loader that loaded the class that needs A, say B, is required to load the class A. This usually takes place in the background, and the only class loader involved is the system class loader. In our case, we have to make our `NodeClassLoader` load the classes of the packet of the migrating object. For this reason, we have to make sure that the received object (contained in the `MigratingPacket`) is actually retrieved by a local object whose class is loaded by the `NodeClassLoader`. Since this class is a local class, i.e., a class present in the local class library, we have to force it to be loaded by the `NodeClassLoader` and not by the system class loader. In particular, the package `mobility` provides an interface, `MigratingCodeRecover` and a class, `MigratingCodeRecoverImpl`, for recovering objects and classes from a `MigratingPacket`. The steps to perform are: load the `MigratingCodeRecoverImpl` class through the class loader (by forcing its loading so to avoid it is loaded by the system class loader) and recover the received packet through the `MigratingCodeRecoverImpl` instance:

```
NodeClassLoader classloader = class_loader_factory.createNodeClassLoader();
String recover_name =
 "org.mikado.imc.mobility.MigratingCodeRecoverImpl";
MigratingCodeRecover recover =
(MigratingCodeRecover) (classloader.forceLoadClass(recover_name).newInstance());
```

Notice that `recover` is declared as `MigratingCodeRecover` but its actual class is `MigratingCodeRecoverImpl` (which is a class implementing the interface `MigratingCodeRecover`). Indeed, the following code would generate a `ClassCast-Exception`:

```
MigratingCodeRecoverImpl recover =
(MigratingCodeRecoverImpl) (classloader.forceLoadClass(recover_name).newInstance());
```

since Java considers two classes loaded with different class loader as incompatible. In the wrong code snippet above, for instance, the class `MigratingCodeRecoverImpl` of the variable `recover` would be loaded through the system class loader, and it would be assigned an object of the same class `MigratingCodeRecoverImpl`, but loaded with `NodeClassLoader`. This is the reason why we have to assign the instance loaded by `NodeClassLoader` to a variable declared with a superclass of the actually loaded class.

Once this `MigratingCodeRecover` object is loaded through our `NodeClassLoader`, we can deserialize the received object with these two simple instructions:

```
recover.set_packet(pack);
MigratingCode code = recover.recover();
```

The method `recover` will return the object stored in the `MigratingPacket` and the classes needed by such object, stored in the packet, will be automatically loaded by the `NodeClassLoader`. We would like to point out that not all the classes of the received object are necessarily loaded immediately; however, each time such object needs a class to be loaded, this request will be handled transparently by the `NodeClassLoader`. We observe that once the object is recovered from a packet, it can be used to create another packet to be sent to another site.

By default, the `JavaByteCodeUnMarshaller` uses a brand new class loader (through an abstract factory) for each `MigratingPacket`. Thus, each migrating object will be incompatible with other migrating objects, since each one of them is loaded through a different classloader. This name space separation provides a sort of isolation that helps avoiding that migrating objects coming from different sites interfere with each other. If this is not the desired behavior, the `JavaByteCodeUnMarshaller` can be initialized with a specific `NodeClassLoader` instance that will always be used to load every migrating object. Alternatively, the user can provide the `JavaByteCodeUnMarshaller` with a customized abstract factory in order to force it to use a customized `NodeClassLoader` for each migrating object.

3   Examples

Let us now show a small tutorial on how to use this package for Java byte-code migrating code. First of all the classes of objects we want to migrate must be subclasses of `JavaMigratingCode`:

```
public class MyCode extends JavaMigratingCode {
 MyVar v = new MyVar();

 public MyRetType getFoo(MyPar p) {...}
 ...
}
```

Now an object of this class (or of one of its possible subclasses) can be sent to a remote site by creating a `MigratingPacket`, through a `JavaByteCodeMarshaller` described above. Once such a packet is created, it can be directly written into an `ObjectOutputStream` that, in turn, is connected, for instance, to a network output stream:

```
public class Sender {
   ...
   void sendCode(OutputStream os) throws Exception {
   MigratingCodeMarshaller marshaller = new JavaByteCodeMarshaller();
   MigratingCode code = new MyCode();
   MigratingPacket pack = marshaller.marshal(code);
   ObjectOutputStream obj_os = new ObjectOutputStream(os);
   obj_os.writeObject(pack);
   obj_os.flush();
   }
}
```

Let us observe that the act of creating a `MigratingPacket` automatically collects all the classes that `MyCode` uses, apart from creating an array of bytes representing the state of the object to migrate. Thus, the classes `MyVar`, `MyRetType` and `MyPar` are stored in the packet as well.

The site that receives a migrating object will basically perform the complementary operations: read a `MigratingPacket` from a stream (e.g., from the network) and use a `JavaByteCodeUnMarshaller` to retrieve the object from the received packet (all the operations for loading the classes will be transparent to the programmer):

```
public class Receiver {
   ...
   JavaMigratingCode receiveCode(InputStream is) throws Exception {
   MigratingCodeUnMarshaller unmarshaller = new JavaByteCodeUnMarshaller();
   ObjectInputStream obj_is = new ObjectInputStream(ss);
   MigratingPacket pack = (MigratingPacket) obj_is.readObject();
   return (JavaMigratingCode) unmarshaller.unmarshal(pack);
   }
}
```

Notice that the object retrieved from the packet is of type `JavaMigratingCode`, thus only the methods defined in that class can be used (e.g., the method `start`, inherited by `Thread`). Moreover a cast to its actual class (that in this example is MyCode) is not possible because that class is unknown in the receiving site and, even if it was known such cast would make the system class loader try to load the class `MyCode`; either the system class loader fails to load the class or, however, the two instances would be incompatible as explained above.

This may seem a strong limitation, but the applications that exchange code can agree on a richer interface or base class for the migrating code, say `MyMigratingProcess`, with other methods, say m and n; such class must be present in all the sites where these applications are running so that it can be loaded by the system class loader. For this reason, the class `MyMigratingProcess` must not be inserted in the `MigratingPacket`. The class `JavaMigratingCode` provides a method, `setExcludeClasses` that allows to specify which classes must not be inserted in the packet[1]. Thus, the code of the sender shown above should be changed as follows (it delivers a `MyProcess` object,

---

[1] We remind that the `mobility` package already excludes all the Java system classes and the classes of the `mobility` package itself.

where MyProcess inherits from the common base class MyMigratingProcess that in turns derives from JavaMigratingCode):

public class Sender {
```
  ...
  void sendCode(OutputStream os) throws Exception {
  JavaMigratingCode code = new MyProcess();
  code.setExcludeClasses("mypackage.MyMigratingProcess");
  MigratingPacket pack = code.make_packet();
  ObjectOutputStream obj_os = new ObjectOutputStream(os);
  obj_os.writeObject(pack);
  obj_os.flush();
  }
}
```

The receiving code can then assign the retrieved object to a MyMigratingProcess instance and then use the richer interface of MyMigratingProcess:

```
MyMigratingProcess code = (MyMigratingProcess) unmarshaller.unmarshal();
code.m();
code.n();
```

An alternative to setExcludeClasses is the method addExcludePackage that allows to exclude a whole package (or several packages) from the set of classes that are delivered together with a migrating object. For instance, the call to setExcludeClasses above could be replaced by the following statement:

```
code.addExcludePackage("mypackage.");
```

This allows to enforce that the whole excluded package is available on all the sites where the migrating code is dispatched to.

When extending JavaMigratingCode, there is an important detail to know in order to avoid run-time errors that would take place at remote sites and would be very hard to discover: Java Reflection API is unable to inspect local variables of methods. This implies that if a process uses a class only to declare a variable in a method, this class will not be collected and thus, when the process executes that method on a remote site, a ClassNotFoundException may be thrown. This limitation is due to the specific implementation of Java Reflection API, but it can be easily dealt with, once the programmer is aware of the problem.

The package provides other functionalities to further customize the behavior of code mobility (for instance the code of an object of a derived class of JavaMigratingCode can be excluded from the class collection procedure by invoking the method setDeliverCode(false). We refer to the documentation of the package for a complete description of all the functionalities.

4   Conclusions

We have presented a Java package that aims at providing a framework for implementing mobile code based distributed applications. and mobile code languages and calculi. The programmer is relieved by all the details of code collection, marshalling and unmarshalling, since code mobility is transparently dealt with by the package itself. The programmer can then concentrate on those parts that are really specific of his system, while relying on the mobility package mobility of code.

In order to experiment the usability of the package (and, more in general, of the IMC framework) we re-engineered the package KLAVA [6,3] so that it uses the mobility package to deal with code mobility. This resulted in a simplification of the overall package since we could completely remove all the mobility parts from KLAVA, by relying entirely on the functionalities provided by the package mobility. Furthermore, we are using the IMC framework to develop a Java run-time system for other mobile calculi.

Acknowledgements

I am grateful to the other authors of the IMC package [4] for their indispensable effort and cooperation during all the stages of design and implementation of the IMC framework.

References

1. A. Acharya, M. Ranganathan, and J. Saltz. Sumatra: A Language for Resource-aware Mobile Programs. In J. Vitek and C. Tschudin [17], pages 111–130.
2. K. Arnold, J. Gosling, and D. Holmes. *The Java Programming Language*. Addison-Wesley, 3rd edition, 2000.
3. L. Bettini. *Linguistic Constructs for Object-Oriented Mobile Code Programming & their Implementations*. PhD thesis, Dip. di Matematica, Università di Siena, 2003. Available at http://music.dsi.unifi.it.
4. L. Bettini, R. De Nicola, D. Falassi, M. Lacoste, L. Lopes, L. Oliveira, H. Paulino, and V. Vasconcelos. A Software Framework for Rapid Prototyping of Run-Time Systems for Mobile Calculi. In *Global Computing*, LNCS. Springer, 2004. To appear.
5. L. Bettini, R. De Nicola, G. Ferrari, and R. Pugliese. Interactive Mobile Agents in X-KLAIM. In *Proc. WETICE*, pages 110–115. IEEE, 1998.
6. L. Bettini, R. De Nicola, and R. Pugliese. KLAVA: a Java Package for Distributed and Mobile Applications. *Software - Practice and Experience*, 32(14):1365–1394, 2002.
7. G. Cabri, L. Leonardi, and F. Zambonelli. Reactive Tuple Spaces for Mobile Agent Coordination. In Rothermel and Hohl [15], pages 237–248.
8. C. Fournet and L. Maranget. The Join-Calculus Language, 1997. Software and documentation available from http://join.inria.fr/.
9. E. Gamma, R. Helm, R. Johnson, and J. Vlissides. *Design Patterns: Elements of Reusable Object-Oriented Software*. Addison-Wesley, 1995.
10. D. Lange and M. Oshima. *Programming and Deploying Java Mobile Agents with Aglets*. Addison-Wesley, 1998.
11. L. Lopes. *On the Design and Implementation of a Virtual Machine for Process Calculi*. PhD thesis, University of Porto, 1999.
12. H. Peine and T. Stolpmann. The Architecture of the Ara Platform for Mobile Agents. In *Proc. MA*, number 1219 in LNCS, pages 50–61. Springer, 1997.
13. G. Picco. μCODE: A Lightweight and Flexible Mobile Code Toolkit. In Rothermel and Hohl [15], pages 160–171.
14. G. Picco, A. Murphy, and G.-C. Roman. LIME: Linda Meets Mobility. In D. Garlan, editor, *Proc. ICSE'99*, pages 368–377. ACM Press, 1999.

15. K. Rothermel and F. Hohl, editors. *Proc. of the 2nd Int. Workshop on Mobile Agents*, number 1477 in LNCS. Springer-Verlag, 1998.
16. D. Sangiorgi and A. Valente. A Distributed Abstract Machine for Safe Ambients. In *Proc. ICALP'01*, volume 2076 of *LNCS*, pages 408–420. Springer-Verlag, 2001.
17. J. Vitek and C. Tschudin, editors. *Mobile Object Systems: Towards the Programmable Internet*, number 1222 in LNCS. Springer, 1997.

Dependability-Explicit Computing:
Applications in e-Science and Virtual Organisations

John Fitzgerald

Abstract. Providing a predictable level of dependability is a challenge for applications which choreograph services from many different providers. Applications commonly fail because a component service fails, yet the designers of applications have, at best, limited information about component service dependability. This limits their ability to make informed decisions about when it is cost-effective to use a service or to employ potentially expensive fault containment or tolerance techniques such as redundancy. We consider ways to improve support for the publication and exploitation of dependability metadata for services by developing publication methods and ontologies to support shared metadata definitions. Two diverse examples of metadata are considered: service availability information and descriptions of service failure modes. The availability work is particularly relevant to bioinformatics, while work on failure modes is explored in the context of virtual organisations with long-term interactions.

About the Speaker. John Fitzgerald is a reader in Computing Science and a member of the Centre for Software Reliability at the University of Newcastle, UK. His research centres on the development of predictably dependable computer-based systems, especially through the judicious application of rigorous methods and tools. For all of his career, John has been working in or with the industry, especially the aerospace sector. In 2003 he returned to academia after establishing design and validation activities at Transitive, a successful new company in the embedded processor market. John is Chairman of the main European body bringing together researchers and practitioners in rigorous methods of systems development (Formal Methods Europe).

N. Guelfi et al. (Eds.): FIDJI 2004, LNCS 3409, p. 123, 2005.
© Springer-Verlag Berlin Heidelberg 2005

Towards a Precise UML-Based Development Method

Gianna Reggio

Abstract. The talk will present an attempt, perhaps unorthodox, at bridging the gap between the use of formal techniques and the current software engineering practices. After years of full immersion in the development and use of formal techniques, we have been led to suggest a strategy, better marrying the rigour of formalities to the needs and, why not, the wisdom of current practices, that essentially aims at proposing methods where the formalities provide the foundational rigour, and perhaps may inspire new techniques, but are kept hidden from the user.

In a stream of papers we have outlined a development method – following that strategy – which is Model-Driven and adopts the UML notation. Here, we will outline in summary such method, briefly covering the phases of domain modelling, requirement specification and the Model-driven Design (or Platform Independent Design). Moreover, in this talk we will show how the proposed method may take advantage of the new and of the improved diagrams of UML 2.0.

About the Speaker. Gianna Reggio got a degree in Mathematics (1981, University of Genova), and after a Ph.D. in Computer Science (1988, Consortium of the Universities of Pisa-Genova-Udine) she started working as a scientific collaborator on various national and international projects, among them the European Project "The Draft Formal Definition of Ada"; then in 1989 she got a position as a Researcher at the University of Genova, and till 1992 she is Associate professor at the same university. She is a member of the IFIP WG 1.3 (Foundations of System Specifications).

The main areas of her research activity have been formal specification and modelling of concurrent systems and semantics of programming languages, and software development methods.

In particular she has developed: formal specification methods for concurrent systems, visual notations grounded in formal specifications, techniques for making "precise" UML, and "precise" software development methods based on UML. Recently, she has been working on development methods specialized for particular domains and/or particular applications (e.g., Web Applications, Enterprise Applications, per-to-peer systems), using as modelling notation either UML or new specifically designed visual and formal specification languages.

N. Guelfi et al. (Eds.): FIDJI 2004, LNCS 3409, p. 124, 2005.

Fault Tolerance – Concepts and Implementation Issues

Jörg Kienzle

Abstract. This tutorial presents an overview of the techniques that can be used by developers to produce software that can tolerate design faults and faults of the surrounding environment, and it offers an introduction on how such techniques can be implemented in a standard programming language. After reviewing the basic terms and concepts of fault tolerance, the most well-known fault-tolerance techniques exploiting software-, information- and time redundancy are presented, classified according to the kind of concurrency they support. The tutorial then concentrates on a specific technique for achieving fault tolerance using backward error recovery: transactions. Transactions group together a set of operations and give them the so-called ACID properties: Atomicity, Consistency, Isolation and Durability. After presenting different transaction models, pessimistic and optimistic concurrency control, and different ways of performing crash recovery are reviewed. Finally, the design of an object-oriented framework that provides support for open multithreaded transactions is outlined. The framework offers different interfaces for application programmers: a procedural, an object-based, an object-oriented and an aspect-oriented one. The interfaces are presented in detail, and their advantages and disadvantages are analyzed.

About the Speaker. Jörg Kienzle is an Assistant Professor at the School of Computer Science, McGill University, Montreal, Canada, where he is leading the software engineering laboratory. He holds a Ph.D. and engineering diploma from the Swiss Federal Institute of Technology (EPFL) in Lausanne. His current research interests include fault tolerance, software development methods, and aspect-orientation. In his Ph.D. thesis, he designed and implemented an object-oriented framework that provides transaction support for programming languages. He was a keynote speaker on "Software Fault Tolerance" at the Reliable Software Technologies - Ada Europe 2003 conference in Toulouse.

N. Guelfi et al. (Eds.): FIDJI 2004, LNCS 3409, p. 125, 2005.
© Springer-Verlag Berlin Heidelberg 2005

Author Index

Lecture Notes in Computer Science

For information about Vols. 1–3306

please contact your bookseller or Springer

Vol. 3353: J. Hromkovič, M. Nagl, B. Westfechtel (Eds.), Graph-Theoretic Concepts in Computer Science. XI, 404 pages. 2004.

Vol. 3352: C. Blundo, S. Cimato (Eds.), Security in Communication Networks. XI, 381 pages. 2005.

Vol. 3350: M. Hermenegildo, D. Cabeza (Eds.), Practical Aspects of Declarative Languages. VIII, 269 pages. 2005.

Vol. 3349: B.M. Chapman (Ed.), Shared Memory Parallel Programming with Open MP. X, 149 pages. 2005.

Vol. 3348: A. Canteaut, K. Viswanathan (Eds.), Progress in Cryptology - INDOCRYPT 2004. XIV, 431 pages. 2004.

Vol. 3347: R.K. Ghosh, H. Mohanty (Eds.), Distributed Computing and Internet Technology. XX, 472 pages. 2004.

Vol. 3346: R.H. Bordini, M. Dastani, J. Dix, A.E.F. Seghrouchni (Eds.), Programming Multi-Agent Systems. XIV, 249 pages. 2005. (Subseries LNAI).

Vol. 3345: Y. Cai (Ed.), Ambient Intelligence for Scientific Discovery. XII, 311 pages. 2005. (Subseries LNAI).

Vol. 3344: J. Malenfant, B.M. Østvold (Eds.), Object-Oriented Technology. ECOOP 2004 Workshop Reader. VIII, 215 pages. 2005.

Vol. 3342: E. Şahin, W.M. Spears (Eds.), Swarm Robotics. IX, 175 pages. 2005.

Vol. 3341: R. Fleischer, G. Trippen (Eds.), Algorithms and Computation. XVII, 935 pages. 2004.

Vol. 3340: C.S. Calude, E. Calude, M.J. Dinneen (Eds.), Developments in Language Theory. XI, 431 pages. 2004.

Vol. 3339: G.I. Webb, X. Yu (Eds.), AI 2004: Advances in Artificial Intelligence. XXII, 1272 pages. 2004. (Subseries LNAI).

Vol. 3338: S.Z. Li, J. Lai, T. Tan, G. Feng, Y. Wang (Eds.), Advances in Biometric Person Authentication. XVIII, 699 pages. 2004.

Vol. 3337: J.M. Barreiro, F. Martin-Sanchez, V. Maojo, F. Sanz (Eds.), Biological and Medical Data Analysis. XI, 508 pages. 2004.

Vol. 3336: D. Karagiannis, U. Reimer (Eds.), Practical Aspects of Knowledge Management. X, 523 pages. 2004. (Subseries LNAI).

Vol. 3335: M. Malek, M. Reitenspieß, J. Kaiser (Eds.), Service Availability. X, 213 pages. 2005.

Vol. 3334: Z. Chen, H. Chen, Q. Miao, Y. Fu, E. Fox, E.-p. Lim (Eds.), Digital Libraries: International Collaboration and Cross-Fertilization. XX, 690 pages. 2004.

Vol. 3333: K. Aizawa, Y. Nakamura, S. Satoh (Eds.), Advances in Multimedia Information Processing - PCM 2004, Part III. XXXV, 785 pages. 2004.

Vol. 3332: K. Aizawa, Y. Nakamura, S. Satoh (Eds.), Advances in Multimedia Information Processing - PCM 2004, Part II. XXXVI, 1051 pages. 2004.

Vol. 3331: K. Aizawa, Y. Nakamura, S. Satoh (Eds.), Advances in Multimedia Information Processing - PCM 2004, Part I. XXXVI, 667 pages. 2004.

Vol. 3330: J. Akiyama, E.T. Baskoro, M. Kano (Eds.), Combinatorial Geometry and Graph Theory. VIII, 227 pages. 2005.

Vol. 3329: P.J. Lee (Ed.), Advances in Cryptology - ASIACRYPT 2004. XVI, 546 pages. 2004.

Vol. 3328: K. Lodaya, M. Mahajan (Eds.), FSTTCS 2004: Foundations of Software Technology and Theoretical Computer Science. XVI, 532 pages. 2004.

Vol. 3327: Y. Shi, W. Xu, Z. Chen (Eds.), Data Mining and Knowledge Management. XIII, 263 pages. 2005. (Subseries LNAI).

Vol. 3326: A. Sen, N. Das, S.K. Das, B.P. Sinha (Eds.), Distributed Computing - IWDC 2004. XIX, 546 pages. 2004.

Vol. 3325: C.H. Lim, M. Yung (Eds.), Information Security Applications. XI, 472 pages. 2005.

Vol. 3323: G. Antoniou, H. Boley (Eds.), Rules and Rule Markup Languages for the Semantic Web. X, 215 pages. 2004.

Vol. 3322: R. Klette, J. Žunić (Eds.), Combinatorial Image Analysis. XII, 760 pages. 2004.

Vol. 3321: M.J. Maher (Ed.), Advances in Computer Science - ASIAN 2004. Higher-Level Decision Making. XII, 510 pages. 2004.

Vol. 3320: K.-M. Liew, H. Shen, S. See, W. Cai (Eds.), Parallel and Distributed Computing: Applications and Technologies. XXIV, 891 pages. 2004.

Vol. 3319: D. Amyot, A.W. Williams (Eds.), System Analysis and Modeling. XII, 301 pages. 2005.

Vol. 3318: E. Eskin, C. Workman (Eds.), Regulatory Genomics. VIII, 115 pages. 2005. (Subseries LNBI).

Vol. 3317: M. Domaratzki, A. Okhotin, K. Salomaa, S. Yu (Eds.), Implementation and Application of Automata. XII, 336 pages. 2005.

Vol. 3316: N.R. Pal, N.K. Kasabov, R.K. Mudi, S. Pal, S.K. Parui (Eds.), Neural Information Processing. XXX, 1368 pages. 2004.

Vol. 3315: C. Lemaître, C.A. Reyes, J.A. González (Eds.), Advances in Artificial Intelligence - IBERAMIA 2004. XX, 987 pages. 2004. (Subseries LNAI).

Vol. 3314: J. Zhang, J.-H. He, Y. Fu (Eds.), Computational and Information Science. XXIV, 1259 pages. 2004.

Vol. 3313: C. Castelluccia, H. Hartenstein, C. Paar, D. Westhoff (Eds.), Security in Ad-hoc and Sensor Networks. VIII, 231 pages. 2005.

Vol. 3312: A.J. Hu, A.K. Martin (Eds.), Formal Methods in Computer-Aided Design. XI, 445 pages. 2004.

Vol. 3311: V. Roca, F. Rousseau (Eds.), Interactive Multimedia and Next Generation Networks. XIII, 287 pages. 2004.

Vol. 3310: U.K. Wiil (Ed.), Computer Music Modeling and Retrieval. XI, 371 pages. 2005.

Vol. 3309: C.-H. Chi, K.-Y. Lam (Eds.), Content Computing. XII, 510 pages. 2004.

Vol. 3308: J. Davies, W. Schulte, M. Barnett (Eds.), Formal Methods and Software Engineering. XIII, 500 pages. 2004.

Vol. 3307: C. Bussler, S.-k. Hong, W. Jun, R. Kaschek, D.. Kinshuk, S. Krishnaswamy, S.W. Loke, D. Oberle, D. Richards, A. Sharma, Y. Sure, B. Thalheim (Eds.), Web Information Systems - WISE 2004 Workshops. XV, 277 pages. 2004.